Death
What is it?

Jane Halliwell Green

Cover Design by Emily Grace Knade

ISBN:1974426203
ISBN-13:9781974426201

DEDICATION

To my mother - Catherine Connolly Halliwell, Born: September 12, 1927- Died: September 2, 2016

Understanding God's plan for your life should, on the one hand, elicit such gratitude in your heart towards such a good father that you would lavish continual thanks to your heavenly benefactor. On the other hand, understanding his plan should strengthen you to refuse to halt your journey because of the pain and sorrow we must endure to reach the end of this very long road.

The Lord told me he revealed these things about his plan to you primarily so you would not be in doubt about the course of your life. Run the course, do not grow weary, run, and may we all run in such a way that, at the end of the journey, we can say with the holy apostle, "I am already on the point of being sacrificed; the time of my departure has come. I have fought the good fight, I have finished the race, and I have kept the faith. "{Timothy 4: 6-7} a letter written by St. Padre Pio on November 26, 1914.

CONTENTS

ACKNOWLEDGMENTS

I am deeply grateful to my husband Donald Green for assisting me in the editing of this manuscript. Special thanks to my niece, Emily Knade who designed and created the cover of this book. Blessings to all of you who contributed questions and listened to my speeches about the subject of death the last couple of years.

Many Blessings,
Jane

FORWARD

"The process of dying is falling asleep. The process of death is waking up." J. Adam Snyder

One Sunday morning as I was sitting in church waiting for the service to begin Saint Germain sat down next to me. I knew it was Saint Germain because I am comfortable and familiar with his vibration which feels like a combination of heat and pressure on my body. I said, "Is that you Saint Germain? He answered, "Yes, we are going to write another book – Death, What Is It?" I said okay, and then my second thought was, oh no-- a book is a lot of work. I always accept the task when Saint Germain makes a request. I hope this book brings great peace to you, especially if you ponder the question, Death What Is It?

Death is a great illusion. It isn't real! Neither is life in a body. This book answers questions about death so we will understand the journey out of the body as well as our births. Death seems as elusive as opposed to the body seemingly so solid, yet the soul is invisible. Thus, where does our soul go when the body is gone? What does the soul look like? Is there a new light body to replace the physical form? All these questions and more are answered in this book. Moreover, many of the personal stories of death focus on the experience after leaving the body and explain the process of death for different people dying in various ways.

We experience three levels of awareness. These are sleep, awake, and death. I asked Saint Germain to talk about our awareness in these three states. He said, "One's

1

awareness after death is enhanced. There is a knowing which envelops all your senses. Within a body you are limited. In heaven all is perceived as an energetic force which is the unconditional love of God, spiritual guides, angels, and Masters like me. You are fully aware. In a body you are asleep. This is why you are encouraged to pay attention as life unfolds around you. Begin detaching from the physical experience. Do not partake of it all day. Use your earth time to make contact with the higher vibrations." I said it sounds as if we are more awake in heaven, and he answered, "Yes, everything is more vivid." I asked if we still have free will. He answered, "Yes, here free will is understood in a profound way. It is a gift given to all souls upon birth."

Saint Germain continues to say, "The interplay between life and death is like a play – we are always changing our costumes. Birth is much scarier than death! The soul slips into form with some difficulty, but out of form easily."

1 ALL THE WORLD, A STAGE

"My home is in heaven. I am just passing through this world," Billy Graham

When you think of death see yourself as an actor or actress on the stage. The stage represents your physical lives. This is where you are now. You are always acting, and at the same time using some improvisation when necessary. Behind the curtain is a large staff supporting you! When the show is over, and the curtain comes down, the support staff comes forward to congratulate you on your performance. Saint Germain likes this analogy and comments, "You are performing for an audience in this physical experience are, you not?" He went on to say, "On the other side there is no need to perform in order to hide who you are, as all aspects of your life and soul are revealed to everyone." This statement should remind us to remove the masks we wear during our physical lives. This mask is not who we really are. It seems appropriate that I am writing this book with Saint Germain who in a previous life was the great bard, Shakespeare. He wrote the great poem:

All the world's a stage,
And all the men and women merely players;
They have their exits and their entrances,
And one man in his time plays many parts,
His acts being seven ages. At first, the infant,
Mewling and puking in the nurse's arms;
And then the whining schoolboy, with his satchel
And shining morning face, creeping like snail
Unwillingly to school. And then the lover,
Sighing like furnace, with a woeful ballad

Made to his mistress' eyebrow. Then a soldier,
Full of strange oaths, and bearded like the bard,
Jealous in honor, sudden and quick in quarrel,
Seeking the bubble reputation.
Even in the cannon's mouth. And then the justice,
In fair round belly with good capon lined,
With eyes severe and beard of formal cut,
Full of wise saws and modern instances;
And so he plays his part. The sixth age shifts
Into the lean and slippered pantaloon,
With spectacles on nose and pouch on side;
His youthful hose, well saved, a world too wide
For his shrunk shank, and his big manly voice,
Turning again toward childish treble, pipes
And whistles in his sound. Last scene of all,
That ends this strange eventful history,
is second childishness and mere oblivion;
Sans teeth, sans eyes, sans taste, sans everything.

Years ago I had a powerful dream. Dreams often contain hidden messages. In my dream I was sitting in a school bus filled with lots of other children. The bus was traveling on a road parallel to a very wide river. I noticed as I looked out the window there were people building boats along the river. I disembarked from the bus and walked down to the edge of the river. Suddenly, I became a man putting the finishing touches on my boat. I saw myself pushing the boat into the river and jumping into it. At that moment I clearly heard a voice shout out to me, "You must build many boats before you can enter the stream of life." I wrote this dream down and tucked it away in my file cabinet. Recently I came across my notes. The meaning of the dream seemed very obvious to me. The boats represent our many bodies. The flowing river represents the

4

movement and emotion of life. There are many rocks in this river. Each rock represents a challenge on the journey up the river. How we maneuver around these rocks is important. We don't want to damage our boat which is a symbol of our bodies. The body is sacred. Finally, the river empties into the ocean and as ocean and river merge together we understand we are everlasting souls not bodies. We are connected to all souls. Every night as we dream we experience this out of body state; we embrace the same feeling of being free of the body. Can you remember moments when you are waking up and became aware of no feeling or sensation in your body? I often think this must be the way it feels when we are free of our bodies.

When I asked Saint Germain to comment on this dream he said the following, "this dream represents the experience of being in the flesh; to maneuver through dense energy, respect the space of others, and find the ocean of God. You must practice forgiveness, as all souls are contained in the same river." Understand in life we have the gift of choice. Many choose to paddle upstream against the current. Life is much easier if we simply follow the choreographed play, float downstream, and follow the script we have written.

I wrote this book because Saint Germain asked me to do it. He chose the topic and the chapter headings. When I heard his instructions regarding the book my first reaction was to say no. There have been so many books written about death --why would we need another? He said this one would be different. As I approach the completion of the manuscript, I can agree with him. The book is personal. It's about you. It also contains stories of world events when many souls perish together. I expect it will bring peace to many of my readers who may be asking the question—Death, what is it?

2 MEANING OF DEATH

Great Spirit, when we face the sunset, when we come singing the last song, may it be without shame, singing it is finished in beauty. It is finished in beauty. Evelyn Eaton

Does consciousness survive death?

One day, I asked Saint Germain, "What is the meaning of death?" He answered me by saying this, "There is no special meaning. It is simply part of the evolution of one as a non-physical being, and the necessity of moving higher on the scale of understanding; knowing your connection with your Source/God. You follow the path of full return to the light, and ultimately to provide service to humanity."

I asked Saint Germain, if the mind survives death? He answered, "Yes, indeed. The conscious mind is rapidly directed to a new life and actively joins the higher energy of the spiritual realm." I continued with my questioning. "So, consciousness is not contained in the brain. Is this correct?" He answered, "Yes, you are correct. Consciousness is who you are! The brain is part of the body." I continued to ask, "Then our consciousness is our mind? He answered, "Yes, the upper mind. The mind with all physical attachments released." I replied, "Consciousness survives death?" Is this correct?" He answered, "Yes, you are eternal. Death is your birthright and necessary in order to acquire experience.

Consciousness is electrical energy. It can change form but will not disappear. It is part of your soul – the invisible energy which animates and activates the soul. One must have consciousness to live within the human form. Death releases your soul and therefore also your consciousness. Every living being has consciousness. This is the law of energy. Experience in a physical environment expands your understanding of who you are. To avoid death would be stagnation. As birth is an exciting adventure, so is death. And the cycle continues."

I asked, "Is death just a stepping stone bringing us closer and closer to a place in our evolution to be of service to others?" He said I was correct and blessed me for my true assessment of his words. One of the great Indian Masters said, "If death were the end, and there is no God, and there are no realized Masters, it is all a pack of lies."

I commented, "Life is very short. We get to the age of 70, and just as we are becoming proficient in our life's work it is almost over. Some people never discover their soul's purpose; other souls find it during the last third of their life. Doesn't this seem a little unfair?"

He laughed and said, "Yes, I see your dilemma. All knowledge and wisdom accumulates. It does not leave you or fly away. The soul contains the skills acquired in every life. When you arrive here you have a sense of knowing the whole and for some individuals it is more than they can handle. There are souls who assist you in seeing all levels of skill, and determining their best use. Do not despair in thinking you lose everything, for instead you gain it all?"

His words bring me peace. I continued on the topic and asked, "Is one lifetime like a single class"? He laughed and said "Yes, and no. One life can be the learning of one lesson or one subject, or it can be a rapid acceleration from the first to the seventh grade. It depends on the goal of the soul and the way their personal plan evolves within the physical experience. Some souls forget the plan and others are driven to achieve."

I asked if it mattered whether somebody was an old or young soul in respect to how quickly they would move through all their lives.

He said, "No, very young souls can be high achievers- just like old ones. Life choices are more important and will result in rapid growth during the physical experience rather than soul age."

I asked, "Could you give me a Definition of soul age?" He said, "Soul age is not measured in the number of lives, but the content of one's lives. The Council of Elders determines a soul's readiness for Ascension."

When we reach the level of Ascension it is no longer necessary to return to a physical body. Ascension represents another cycle of growth but all done at the higher vibrations beyond the dense energy of the physical world.

I asked Saint Germain if going to war is a death wish?

He answered, No, "It is not. Going to war is simply forced upon the soul by the society with which he or she belongs. Those who choose the experience rarely consider the consequences of the choice, because most souls do not believe they will transition early."

I found his comment about the lack of fear and consequences in choosing to go to war fascinating. I continued to ask for more information. What happens to a soldier who does not anticipate death and ends up dying after a battle? He replied, "It is very difficult for a soul who chose war, and did not anticipate the potential consequences. There are guides who assist with the grief; in handling both the soldier's feelings and the loved ones left behind. These souls often return rapidly to a physical life."

I asked, "Is it a sin to kill the enemy who may be trying to kill me?" He responded, "It is not. Particularly for one who has no understanding of what he has done. Only souls who understand the penalty for taking another's life suffer the consequences. The consequence requires a soul to carry the debt until it is repaid." I asked him if we carry the debt into the next life. He said, "Not necessarily. The elders spend a lot of time with the soul. The debt is reviewed again and again in spirit. One is asked to choose a way to alleviate the penalty. It is a deep and serious conversation with the elders."

I wondered about the possibility of one soul surviving and another dying during battle? He said, "It is simply chance. The soul who survives asks many deep questions such as why me; or the opposite, I am not good as I survived and my friend died. Guides assist these souls."

Most people see death as final. I stated, "Wouldn't it be better if a larger number of people understood they are pure consciousness and could not die?" He responded, "Yes of course." Many religious organizations do not teach truth. Life continues and one returns over and over again to the physical experience. Instead, organized religions imply death is final. For those like you, teaching reincarnation and studying both Eastern and Western religious doctrine, the answer is clear."

I have found past life regression- (being put under hypnosis to relive past lives) to be very powerful in taking away the fear of death. I asked Saint Germain if this powerful practice should be understood and utilized by more people. He said, "Yes indeed. It is now being accepted through the courage of souls who serve as a conduit for the experience. It should be encouraged and offered to those able to handle what can often be an emotional remembrance."

I asked what the spiritual world thinks of the way we handle death here on earth. He replied, "We allow families to decide on the best way to honor their dead. You must honor the soul, not the dead body." I responded, "How does the spiritual world view our practice of burial and the use of a casket?"

He replied, "Over time burials will decrease in number as your population understands the earth is sacred. The land should be used for other purposes. As time progresses the Earth's population will increase and most, out of necessity, will choose the burning of the body. The best way dispose of the body is to return the physical remains to the earth."

He went on to say, "The use of a casket is such a waste. A thing of beauty should be seen." I asked him about hospice care and I found his answer very interesting. He said, "The spiritual world is actively involved with the souls who provide this (end-of-life) service you call hospice care. They are light workers, meaning older souls, who have been prepared for this work since birth."

I asked Saint Germain to explain to me how a soul is born; how it comes into existence?" He responded by saying, "You see, the soul is energy, and as you know, everything in the universe qualifies as energy. The energy from which souls are born is very special. It is created by God. It is unlimited and never dies, except to be returned to the Source from which it came. Only the elders can return energy to the Source. Energy, vibration, and non-physical substance contains the power and heart of each Being (soul) and is unique. It has taken on the characteristics you have given it through lifetimes in many physical worlds. Therefore, it is unique to you. It is a gift given to a baby upon the first birth into form."

I asked, "How is a life measured? In other words, did I beat the world or did it beat me?"

Saint Germain said, "This is a complex question. Life is measured by the degree a soul gives of themselves to others. Nothing is more important. Those who build castles and hoard great stores of gold do not move quickly to a higher level of growth here. We evaluate souls and they also evaluate themselves. When the physical world has been left behind everything looks different. The value of a previous physical experience is quickly seen as only a small stepping stone across a river. One meets with guides and teachers and the life is reviewed in depth. All aspects of serving others are registered here. No event is un-charted. Most souls are surprised to see the intricacies of this chart and they vow to try harder in the future."

I asked, "Do some individuals live longer and remain in their bodies until they pass the age of 100 because their thoughts are more positive?"

He replied, "One who desires to stay will remain in the body longer. One, who gives up, will quickly come here. There are many factors outside of the soul's control affecting the process of departure. For instance, the physical body may not be able to hold the soul for a longer length of time. There is also hesitation in leaving as one waits for family members to be present. It is also possible fear holds the soul back." I asked if the guides supporting the dying person try to remove this fear and he said, "Yes, we work diligently to do so, but fear is a barrier for many."

The cessation of breath frightens me. I asked him if one can die before the breath stops. In our earlier conversations he said, "When there is a terrible accident like a plane crash; the souls are removed before the actual crash." If this is true, the soul would not experience their last breath. Saint Germain explained, "You will continue to have the sensation of breathing until you realize it's unnecessary."

I asked, "What is the astral fog and can we withdraw from the body without it? He said, "This is a substance existing in the space between physical life and eternal life. It is a barrier. It supports the release of the soul by releasing a medicinal potion to calm the soul who is departing." I asked, can we withdraw from the body without the astral fog?" and he said, "Yes, it is used when souls resist the separation of soul from body. Once the cord detaches at the base of the brain there is a sense of euphoria."

Our bodies are always connected to the spiritual world by this cord. During our physical lives we may have outer body experiences during our dreams, but we always snap back into the body since the cord is always secured to the base of the brain until we die. At death it is severed.

I asked Saint Germain if he knew my personal wishes in regards to my death. He answered, "Yes."

Saint Germain says it's very important for us to inform our guides how we want to die. Be sure you have had this important conversation with them!

If your guides don't know your wishes they will decide for you based on their deep knowledge of who you are. Saint Germain continued to say, "Often the soul departs before the final breath, however in some cases, the breath and soul are in union and both depart on the very last breath." He said it is variable but in my case he would bring me home before the last breath because it is my wish.

A popular author of the 19th century taught her students to prepare for death. She said, "Upon sleep we should withdraw our consciousness to the head." Then she said, "See if you can stay aware until you reach the astral plane. Watch how you fall asleep; do you see light, hear noises, and see color. All these are phenomena." She continued, "Death is easier if we become aware of how our body falls asleep." I found this very interesting.

Saint Germain assures us we don't miss breathing and we don't even think about its absence. I asked, "If there is an accident, would we leave our bodies at the perfect time for us?" He said, "Yes, with some exceptions. As we have discussed previously, accidents may occur before we are able to respond. (*By 'we' he is referring to your spiritual team*). In most cases, we choose to leave our bodies at exactly the right time." I continued to question him, "Are we aware we are making this choice?" He said, "Not always. Some fight the decision on a conscious level but have already decided to leave their bodies in their subconscious minds."

Our conscious mind is concerned with the life we are living now. The sub-conscious mind has all the memories of every life we have ever lived and this part of our mind knows what lies on the other side of the veil between life and death!

"Does death release our conscious and subconscious selves? Which is our real identity? Doesn't consciousness last beyond the brain's death?" Saint Germain said, It is a difficult concept and important that we make the answer very clear for those who do not understand the terms. He said, "You are a glorious being composed of many layers. One is awake and aware of the layer which conducts business on a daily basis. This is your consciousness. Do you understand?" I answered, "Yes I do." He continued to say, "Sometimes you are aware of the deeper layers but some souls never access subconscious memories containing information of previous physical lives. The conscious mind is wrapped around the subconscious. Please see it this way; the life just lived becomes part of the whole. This is the new mind once you arrive here in a non-physical environment. You are an extra conscious being with all memories of the current experience and all memories of every life. In heaven we do not allow you to be aware of all your memories until you are ready."

A Personal Story

"We are all concerned about our own mortality. We wonder if our lives have meaning. If death is the end, what meaning does my life have?" Author unknown

Dennis G.

Born July 6, 1949

Died November 10, 2009

Dennis had multiple sclerosis for 25 years and lived until he was 60. He left a wife and three sons. He is my husband Don's twin brother. I met him briefly before we were married.

He was born on July 6, 1949 and his life path number was a 9. His birth number indicates an interest in spirituality, a need for both time alone and outgoing activities, and a love of people in general.

There are many books on numerology written about the meaning of one's birth date.

He died on November 10, 2009 leaving the world on the restless number five. However, the month of November is the 11th month which is a very spiritual number. His day of death indicates a sense of accomplishment.

Saint Germain facilitated this conversation and the first thing I heard Dennis say was, "thank you for calling on me."

Did you die alone or with family?

I died with family present.

What can you say about your illness?

"It was the most difficult challenge I faced while alive as the soul Dennis. I felt picked upon; that I got this illness. I got a bum deal. It isn't fair. Why me? Eventually I became complacent and accepted the illness, but I felt deep sorrow to be a parent without strength and energy. I left too much to my wife Sarah. When I died I was told I had chosen this illness. I could hardly believe it. The elders showed me my agreement."

Jane- I asked Saint Germain if it's possible to have a pre-agreement to take on a serious illness in the physical life.

Saint Germain – "Yes indeed, it is offered to many, however few accept. Those who willingly agree to be handicapped and limited by the physical self grow rapidly in spirit. There is internal soul work accomplished by these individuals. One is forced to go inward and realize the meaning of life; not from the strictly physical sense. One becomes united with their soul. A soul who accepts this challenge willingly removes himself from the cycle of physical life quickly. Dennis has risen to a higher spiritual plain and will be trained to serve those who have chosen a similar life's challenge."

What do you want to say about your own illness?

"I was always supposed to be the funny one and I needed that sense of humor."

Was it a good death?

"Yes, I knew it was coming. I prayed to God to let me go. I prayed every day for release. I love my Sarah and my boys but I was ready to let go of this body."

What was your death like?

"I fell asleep, and the next thing I saw was a tall man with pure white hair." He said, "I am James and I want to welcome you home. You have succeeded in this glorious life. We applaud you." "I saw others coming closer and I recognized my family; my father and stepmother. There was also a baby; the one we lost."

What did your stepmother say to you?

She kissed me and said she came to celebrate my crossing. She begged me to forgive her and I said, "of course I do."

How did you feel when you realized you were still alive but physically dead?

"For the first time in many years, I could feel my hands and toes. I stood up and ran in a circle holding my head. It was a dance of joy. At the same time, I remembered Sarah and Don, the boys, and my friends."

What do you do for fun and pleasure?

"I have been given all the time I need to travel and be active in sports here. I belong to all the sports clubs. I have traveled to Italy where I experienced many lives. I am having fun. The work will come later. They tell me I earned this."

So you're not working?

"No not yet. I will be working with those in earthly bodies, who like me, are ill and gradually will lose their ability to function in their physical bodies."

What did your elders say when you arrived?

They said, "You are an example to others; particularly those who want a rapid progression to the higher place here. It is easy to make the choice before birth, but now as I look back at my agreements, I am startled I took on such a hard life."

Do you connect with your brother Don from the afterlife?

"Yes, but not much now. There is a sense of no time here and he will be here soon enough." (*Don is his twin brother still alive here in the physical world*).

What was the biggest surprise after leaving the body?

"That I am still here!!!! I didn't believe my life would continue past death. I wish I had known. My brother told me this would happen, but I dismissed his words as incredulous."

Do you get to eat or drink anything?

"Yes, there is everything here anyone would like. There is no physical hunger. It is the memories of eating and enjoying the company of others."

Were you able to see your own funeral?

"Yes, and my body being burned; that was the best sight......DONE!!"

I said, there was somebody at the funeral home who thought you were present. They mistook you for your identical twin brother Don.

"Yes. I am so glad Don is okay and happy. I can't wait to give him a tour of this amazing place."

Is there anything else you want to say?

"Thank you for hearing me when I mentioned Disney world to you one day. I never had the time to spend with my boys like I wanted to."

*(**Jane's note** -One day while I was walking my dog I heard a voice. The voice mentioned Disney World and being unable to give his kids that experience. The voice said, "Tell Don I gave the rest of the family an opportunity to grow also – through my illness others had to grow up – both spiritually and physically. My life will be used to help others like myself.")*

Have you seen your brother Rick? (*His brother Rick died a few years before him*).

"Yes, we have spent time together. He is also enjoying the rest. He found some guys who are like himself and study energies unknown to anyone else. He came from the star system called the Pleiades."

3 PREPARATION

"The act of dying is the great universal ritual which governs our entire planetary life, but only in the human family, and faintly, very faintly in the animal kingdom is the reaction to fear found." Author unknown

I asked Saint Germain many questions about preparing to die. "Is it is possible to prepare for death, and if so, what is the best way to prepare?"

He said, "Be un-connected to the physical experience. Those who focus on their soul's purpose and seek the higher knowledge, lose their fear of death. Prepare for what awaits you here." I replied, "Is there sadness, relief or a sense of loss in leaving the body?" He replied, "Most are relieved, but there is sadness for some. All the emotions come to the surface. Souls are deeply saddened in leaving their loved ones, however as you know, separation is only for a moment. Those who are like yourself understand this and leave the body with gratitude for a life well-lived and a new experience ahead."

I asked if there is a door to the afterlife. Saint Germain said, "There is an energetic portal. It is a stream of highly charged energy that forms around those who are in their final hours. There is no door. The opening to these energies is vast. One cannot comprehend! The soul enters at a place of our choosing; where others have gathered to receive him/her. It is all CAREFULLY arranged to assist and help each soul release themselves from the body. It is like changing one's clothes and then the Angels lift the soul outward from within the cavity of the brain. It is very Easy; the soul is simply removed." "Can we remain conscious when we die? I know many of the great Masters are able to choose the exact time of their death?"

He said, "Most souls are unaware of this possibility. Most believe death is something that happens to you, rather than for you. This means you choose the time to depart." I replied, "So it's a matter of choice?" He responded, "Partly. One must decide if they are able to depart. You can see the detachment of the cord from the body. In one's thoughts you are told by your guides to pinch the cord at the base of the brain to release it from the body. In this way the spirit is able to see their true home." I answered, "You make it sound very simple?" He replied, "It is very easy and for you it would be very good as you like to be in control. Is this not correct?"

I had to admit he hit the nail on the head. I like to be in control. I questioned him further as to whether someone could leave too soon; in other words, before their time in the body was complete? He said, "This would not be allowed by those on the other side who guide us. When we pinch the cord at the base of the brain we're doing it in the area where the pineal gland is located."

I asked, "What is a conscious death like? Would you see the tunnel for instance? "Saint Germain said, "One is quickly brought through the lower into the higher vibrations. It is so fast some feel disoriented. Others are quickly home and relieved to have crossed so quickly."

I asked," Do we always enter the afterlife by the same door?" He said, "There are many doors as the universe is vast and earth-based souls enter at various locations. There are other worlds and souls from faraway planets use the same portals."

I wondered if we leave via the solar plexus, head, or possibly both? His answer to this question was very interesting. He said the following; "the head is the exit point for souls who understand the dominant connection point between spirit and form is at the base of the brain. Other souls travel upwards from the lower chakras lifting the energy slowly to the brain and then upwards and out. You will have no fear and will rush home. Those with fear walk very slowly – delaying what they believe is the end of everything."

I asked Saint Germain about Ariel Sharon, former Prime Minister of Israel who was in a coma for eight years before his body died in 2014. Saint Germain said, "The soul left the body." He continued to say, "Because this man was a symbol for his people, the body was kept alive."

I asked if preparation for death is different if one comes from another planet. Saint Germain said, "Yes, only in so far as the body itself is unique. One's spine and brain in the human body are designed for travel in and out of planet Earth. Other bodies have their own unique design. For instance, there is a civilization where souls come and go through the heart center. All body functions are linked to a central axis. In the human body, the brain and spinal cord dominate and is the energetic highway of both motion and separation." I asked, "Why are people afraid of dying and how can this be changed?" He said, "You bring peace to people who are fearful. Continue to teach life is eternal."

Will we know our life is ending? Do angels approach us at

this time?

Angels are often seen by the dying. My mother, just prior to her passing, was visited by the tall angels called the Seraphim. She said they were dressed in lovely colors of pink, blue and violet, and that their heads touched the ceiling of her room. I remember asking her how she felt when she saw them, and she said, "I feel wonderful."

Saint Germain answered, "There is a desire to go home within the inner recesses of the medulla oblongata which is at the base of your brain. It is where the life force of the soul is controlled. The desire to leave grows over time and your guides notify your Council of Elders."

The medulla oblongata is an important part of the brain. Its functions are in voluntary or done without thought. We could not live without it. It sits at the base of the brain. Spiritually, it is the entrance to our life force, sometimes referred to as prana and controls the flow of prana in an out of our bodies.

I told Saint Germain I would like to die consciously. This means I will be alert through the entire process and fully aware of what is happening. He responded, "I will come for you and assist you in crossing over to the higher energies." He went on to say that when I see him I will hold his hand and we will rise together.

I asked, "What happens immediately after the soul leaves the body? Do we stick around or get swept into the spirit world?" He said, "You see what gives you comfort. The experience of leaving the body is very easy. You choose the time and we simply supply the vehicle. You are met by those who await your arrival. There is a celebration and one feels welcomed. There are those who speak to you and your telepathic abilities are enhanced. The journey home is simply that. You have been here before and your guides will work closely with you to assist you in finding your classrooms. Death is the same regardless of the world from which you arrive. Beings living on other planets make the same journey from their physical bodies to spirit."

A Personal Story

Margaret Ann

Died, October, 2014

"I often think people we have loved and who have loved us become part of us and we carry them around all the time-- whether we see them or not. And in some ways, we are a sum total of those who have loved us and those we have given ourselves to." *Anonymous*

Margaret was about 66 years old when she died. She was very ill and had been hospitalized. She died in the operating room. It was a shock to her family and friends because it was thought she would recover and go home. She had just moved into a new apartment and was excited about the change. She and I were old friends dating back to our teens. I called her Peg. This is my conversation with her in spirit.

I love you and thank you for talking to me. I can hear you clearly. I was shocked when you died in surgery and so was the rest of your family. What do you remember about this?

"It was my choice. I did not want my family to see me in such a difficult and diseased body. I asked my guides to let me die. I am excited to talk with you. I love Saint Germain and I'm thrilled to help you with your book."

(She was able to see Saint Germain and I saw her touching his robe.)

"I was ready to leave and especially after my struggle with this body. I knew it was time. I didn't want to create more problems for my family. I just wanted to slip away."

Did you make this decision to leave before you went into the operating room?

"Yes, I asked to be released before they rolled me in. I was hopeful I would not come back."

What happened immediately after you crossed to the other side?

"There were so many people that came to greet me – hundreds – I was so overwhelmed and then I realized I had crossed over and died. I was so happy – best feeling in years. I saw my mom first and she was so comforting. Then I was taken to a comfortable room and told to rest."

Do you remember your actual crossing?

"No, I don't remember. It was as if they rolled me into the operating room, and the next minute I was waking up with all my relatives and friends by my side."

Did you see angels?

"Yes, but not right away. Once the crowd opened up I saw these beautiful lights. The light surrounded me and I felt lighter and floaty."

What happened next?

"I slept. When I woke up there was a lady standing next to me. She hugged me and said she would be my guide to take me to the next step."

How long did you sleep?

"I don't remember."

Have you seen your family on earth?

"No, I am thinking about them now. I wish we had said goodbye, but I know they will manage without me. I am satisfied with my life and I left none too soon."

What are you doing now?

"Resting, traveling, and spending time studying. I have learned so much but I'm afraid I will forget it. I love the music here."

Have you seen your Akashic record?
(This is the record of all our lives and spirit often describes a library where the records are stored).

"Yes, and I keep going back to the library. Some of it is hard to watch. I want to cry or run away. I could have made better choices."

Are you working?

"No, not really." I was told to relax and enjoy myself. There are books to read. The books are like Kindles. As I read the letters move."

Can you see your children?

"Yes, but for short periods of time. I really don't want to

look. They will be here soon and I am at peace."

Were you present at your funeral?

"Not that I can remember, but when I woke up my guides allowed me to hear the words spoken by my friend Trudy."

I am sorry we had an argument about politics and didn't talk for about a year.

"I am so sorry – it was stupid and not important."

Can you eat or drink?

"Yes, there is a place with food and its fun to go there just to talk to the others." We compare our lives and deaths. It's a place to talk and it's reminiscent of a café on earth."

Can you taste the food?

"It's all a mirage but we can taste it. There is no appetite. The body has the cravings. It's the mind that wants to taste something."

Have you thought about returning to another life?

"No. I don't want to leave – not yet. I am in heaven truly. I know there will be another life, but for now I can enjoy this place."

What is the best part of being there?

"There is no pressure – no work. I love having conversations with my new and old friends--- and family."

Do you have a place to live?

"Yes, I have a small apartment. It has a bed and table. I don't live there. I rest there or go there to be alone. I haven't decided where to go yet."

Don't you want to spend time on Cape Cod?
(She loved Cape Cod, Massachusetts).

"Yes, I have considered this. I go back and forth. It feels like the real place but there are no smellies--- but I can put my toes in the ocean."

Note- *What she meant by smellies is probably the strong odor of the seaweed and rocks on the shore of Cape Cod.*

What would you tell other people about this death experience in general?

"Don't be afraid. It is a wonderful release and a beautiful place to live and wander about. There is no pressure except what you take on yourself."

Did you have a life review?

"Yes, my elders showed me the last life from their perspective and then asked for my opinion. We talked a long time. I will be taking classes and preparing for more lives, but it is my choice as when to begin."

Have you seen Mike?
(Mike was my ex-husband. He died about 6 years before her. He and Peggy were good friends.)

"Yes, (She laughed). We have had a few laughs together."

This was the end of our conversation and I sadly said goodbye.

4 DYING

"The greatest mystery of all time is death. The greatest worry for most people along with this is the meaning of life, if life is extinguished."
Princess Diana

Saint Germain says we should see death and disease as liberating. Both are a release; an opportunity to prepare for one's journey home or take charge of the body.

I mentioned "some people believe consciousness could be split as one travels to the astral plane upon death." He said "No, this is not the case, as no soul is alone in taking the journey home. We would never let one's consciousness be split. See death as a liberating process. People fail to Relate death and sleep. Death after all, is only a longer interval outside the physical plane. You have only gone abroad."

I asked, "What kind of signs are given to us signaling our death is near." He replied, "The desire to move on, loss of interest in activities and work, a lack of interest in food and beverages, and finally a need to be alone." He went on to say, "The presence of loved ones in the room delays the process of dying. One can help by encouraging a soul to leave." I found this interesting because we often hear stories about a loved one on their death bed waiting until everybody has left the room before they depart!

I asked, "Is the time of our death known at our birth? In other words, is it programmed?" He said, "No, it is not. There are tasks and experiences to be accomplished in the life. This is most important. You must finish the class and each life is a class. Some souls are in first grade and need 90 years to move to second grade. Some are in graduate school and finish early."

"How can we help people who fear death?" He said, "You help by sharing information they will accept as true. Someone outside of themselves can see the larger picture. The work we do together helps many. The book and lecture will help because you assist souls to release the fear." I responded, "I am told it is not just a fear of death itself, but the process of dying causing most of the fear? This includes the uncertainty, pain, and the final goodbyes." He responded saying, "One always has doubt. It happens in any life-changing situation such as moving to a new place or beginning a new job. Any change can create anxiety. Is this not true?" I answered, "Yes of course, but death is always seen as something so final?" Saint Germain said "It is the same; one can fear the known and the unknown at the same time. You have experienced physical death hundreds of times yet do not remember. There is no blackness here except what you create yourself. The experience is gentle and most souls have left their physical shells many times. Simply release the fear and this will make the impending death very easy."

"Murder is a sin and interferes with the soul's purpose. Is this true?" Saint Germain said, "Yes, the taking of another soul's life will hold the soul back, and there are many occasions where a soul is taken back to the level from which they began." He continued to say; "Sometimes a soul is rehabilitated without success and must be returned to the Universal Pool of Substance. This is the material of the soul." *(A soul can be extinguished but Saint Germain explains it is a very rare occurrence.*)

I will share an experience I had waking up one morning. Before I was completely awake I felt as if I was floating. I had no sense of a body and I thought to myself, this must be the way it feels when we die. Saint Germain reminded me energy cannot be destroyed. He said, "Your experience represents the first step in death when the soul has a sense of floating upwards and cannot sense any part of the physical self. It is a preliminary step. Then, one will become aware of others who are available to assist during the separation of the cord. In your own experience of waking up, you were still linked to the cord." He went on to say the way we experience death is a choice. Some choose to linger and others to leave quickly. He reminded me this is why our spiritual team wants to know what kind of death we desire. I asked him if there was a benefit to a lengthy illness. He said "No, there is none for the person who dies, only for the family and friends in allowing them to adjust to the absence of the loved one."

Jane's note--- I found this fascinating. It made me wonder if we should be encouraging our loved ones to leave quickly by telling them that it's okay to go.

The dying process

People fail to relate death and sleep. Death, after all is only a longer interval in the life of physical plane functioning; one has only "gone abroad" for a longer period. Alice Bailey

Perhaps we should have an awareness of death at all times by seeing every moment of life against a backdrop of death. Would we be more fully alive? We need to be ready to let go.

I asked Saint Germain if he would explain the dying process from beginning to end until the brain stops. He said, "The dying process is unique for each soul. One who is ill prepares themselves within their mind. The thoughts focus primarily on loved ones. As the thoughts move away from the earthly plane, the cord becomes thin. There is a moment when the soul says either openly or silently, "I am ready." There are angels and guides here who respond and sever the cord in preparation to receive the soul. The first step is withdrawal of the life force within the dense physical body. Second, one withdraws the life force from the ethereal body, thirdly, one withdraws the life force from the astral or emotional body, and fourth one withdraws the life force from the mental body."

"Do most people know they are approaching death?" He said, "Yes, those who are incapacitated as a result of physical decline are especially aware. Those who die in accidents are surprised." "I have heard it said, when someone is close to death we can see this around their eyes. There is relaxation and peace in this area of the body. Is this true?" He said, "Yes, however some souls cross so quickly there is no time for the body to relax and prepare for the journey."

"When my mother died she saw very tall angels. Were these the Seraphim?" He said, "Yes indeed. This is a soothing encounter for souls who are allowed to see them. They reach down to the childlike ones."

I understood this completely as my mother was very childlike towards the end of her life and particularly when she approached death.

"My husband's father-in-law saw beautifully colored hot air balloons and felt he was floating. Is this a common experience?" Saint Germain answered, "It is a choice made by the guides assisting a soul on their journey. Some may see Jesus, some see the angels. It is different for each soul. You, Jane, will see me." He went on to say, "A soul's departure is unique. The sense of floating is common as one moves upward and away from the body. Some souls feel this just as a scuba diver feels the pressure reduced as he floats upward to the surface of the water. Others feel as if they are flying."

I asked if we exit from the head and he said this, "First one begins to rest, and this slows down all the bodily functions. There is less desire for company, food, or outside activities or stimuli. Then death is acknowledged by the soul who calls and says I am ready. The body begins to shut down. All doors are locked. The stomach area is one of the first organs to close along with the lower body from the breast downward. The sensation in the legs and feet is quickly diminished. Then one prepares in their mind. There is a final request to go. One's breathing is shallow and some souls are already outside of the body- moving in and out- taking one more look at this body! Then once the cord is clipped, the soul, with the help of their Guardian Angel, slips quickly out of the body from the head area. All energy moves upward to the base of the skull and then outward from the head. Once the soul is free, the spiritual team guides it to the higher energies here."

I asked him if it was the will of the soul which determines the moment of death and he said, "Yes, The

time of departure is controlled by the soul."
I wondered if it was easier for a spiritual medium to cross over and he said, "Yes, it will be very easy for you. Simply ask to go and release yourself to us. You will ask to leave earlier than most knowing the world here is delightful, and you will be free to expand your consciousness. This is only possible outside of the body."

I asked Saint Germain to comment on the fear of death. I was thinking of my own father who never believed he was going to die until his last breath. Saint Germain said, "There are younger souls who only embrace the physical experience. They are unaware of the unseen parts of life. These souls are given a sedative; to be in deep rest and calmness just before departure from the body."

I recall a quote by a monk who counseled dying patients to really give up and actively die. He said, "We die not into death but into a richer life." Saint Germain agreed and said, "Yes indeed, there is a sense of freedom here. One is truly able to explore all aspects of their being. To explore their interests and enjoy all relationships."

"Does over medicating people or the use of life support make it impossible for them to experience their final moments, or prepare for death?" He said, "Yes, when one is in a state of semi-consciousness from the intervention of unnecessary drugs the experience of dying is spoiled. This is a glorious uplifting experience. This cloud created by the use of unnecessary drugs is quickly removed upon arrival here, but it is still a block to having the full experience of dying."

Someone who was contacted by a spiritual medium

after experiencing their death said, "It was like light coming up from the bottom of the pool to the surface." "Is this accurate?" "Yes indeed, very true."

In my work as a spiritual medium I ask my clients for their date of birth. We choose our own birth date with the assistance of our Council of Elders and it is a significant number. Saint Germain said to me, "This is why babies arrive early or late!" Before I do a reading I ask for my client's birth date and check their life path number. It is a symbol we chose before our birth. There are symbols embedded in the number which are clues about the upcoming life. This made me wonder if the date of death also has significance. Saint Germain said, "It is indicative of the experience in the afterlife." I found this amazing. I asked him about my mother. She was born on September 12, 1927 and she died on September 2, 2016. Her life path number was a four which is evidence she would be very attached to the physical experience. Her outgoing death number was a two which is about balance. Saint Germain liked my analogy. He said, "Your mother is expanding her view of the meaning of life. She will begin to understand her soul in this cycle."

(I think this is very true. Even before her death I noticed she was seeing life differently—possibly acknowledging the continuation of life after death).

Saint Germain continued to say there are celebrations and reunions on the higher plains. This is the other side of physical birth. One simply comes home and the energy of this date is a new beginning.

I asked about the way we die. "Do we choose to leave our physical bodies by drowning, falling, suicide, and if so, why would we choose to drown or to fall?" He said, "Somebody who drowns might be caught in a situation and unable to remove themselves. This is considered an accident and we respond to a pre-mature departure of the body. However, we are not always successful in stopping it. One can be in the wrong place at the wrong time." Regarding suicide he comments, "This is a very sad event. We are disappointed when it occurs. Life is sacred and each soul has an opportunity to grow spiritually while in a body. The body is a perfect place to grow. A soul who leaves before their physical life is over is set back on their own soul's journey."

I asked if most deaths were planned. He said, "Yes, the majority of deaths are pre-planned and anticipated, but this is not true for everyone. When there is a spontaneous death, such as a fall, the soul is removed from the body and in most cases the impact and pain of the death is absent."

I learned this a few years ago when there was a terrible accident in the Swiss Alps. A large plane crashed. It was driven directly into the mountain by the pilot. This terrible tragedy upset me and I went directly to Saint Germain to ask him about the fate of the passengers. He said the only thing the passengers knew was they were standing in the rubble of the aircraft surrounded by their guides and angels, and being told what had happened. He said they had been removed from the plane prior to the accident because the spiritual world anticipated the crash. They were shown the first platform (the entry into heaven); and then the group was separated in order to rest and meet with their own spiritual teams. Later, they were re-united. When one dies with others as in this case, there is a special bond. This group meets often here on this side and have become friends."

Saint Germain said this is true for many accidents. The souls never feel the impact because their souls are removed instantly from the body. This was true for 9/11. The souls of individuals who lost their lives were removed prior to their physical bodies feeling the impact of whatever caused their deaths.

A Personal Story

A Near-Death Experience

"Death is just a method of re-focusing energy, prior to a forward moving activity, and always towards the betterment of the soul." Alice Bailey

This is an account of an amazing near-death experience. It was described to me by a lovely lady named Elizabeth. She has given me permission to share it with you. This happened between the months of January and March, 1986. Elizabeth was 30 years old and had two small children at home. Everything was going well in Elizabeth's life. She had a great career and a wonderful husband and two lovely children.

Elizabeth became severely ill and was admitted to a teaching hospital with a rare cancer of the adrenal gland. She was very ill and weighed only 95 pounds. Her blood pressure was 220/130 and her adrenal gland was secreting over 10 times its normal readings. Regardless of the various tests and procedures the doctors tried, they could not stabilize her. There were no MRIs at this time so all her organs were x-rayed by nuclear medicine. This showed the arteries feeding her right kidney had narrowed and this was corrected after an angioplasty. She was in and out of the hospital many times and had numerous surgical procedures.

Just before her fourth exploratory surgery she had a premonition something bad was going to happen. She asked to speak to the hospital chaplain before the surgery. The chaplain asked her, "Why do you want to meet with me?" Elizabeth answered, "I am sick and not sure I'm going to make it this time. I want to ask God for forgiveness." Elizabeth felt the chaplain was surprised by her remarks. She was a young mother and at her age it would be very unlikely that she would die in surgery.

The day of the surgery

On the day of the surgery Elizabeth remembers four men and two women who surrounded her in the surgical suite. This is her account of what happened:

Elizabeth: I felt pulled away from my body and as I looked down at it from above I thought to myself, "Oh my God, that poor soul is going to die. I have to pray for her."

Then suddenly she realized it was her!!! She said there was this sudden moment of fear and almost instantly the fear went away.

Elizabeth: "There was a dark void and it was cold but this was the most beautiful part for me. I felt as if I was pure energy. I knew it was dark on both sides of me. Then I heard myself say, "Oh wow!" The dark void became a tunnel. I saw a light and I slowly floated towards it. I was being pulled towards two silhouettes. I knew that one was a tiny female and the other a male. The light ahead became more beautiful and brilliant the closer I floated towards it."

The tiny female spoke to me and said, "Are you calm?" I answered, "Yes." She spoke to me again and said, "Are you at peace and do you feel safe?" I answered her by saying, "yes, safer than ever before in my life." I felt happy and excited and wanted to be in the light. This male light being (spirit) spoke to me and said, "Do you feel love?" I answered, "Yes." I was happy and so excited to be in this light. He asked me if I felt peace and calm. I answered, "Yes, but please forgive me for my sins." He replied, "There is no forgiveness. It is not needed here. It is not necessary. Do you want to stay?" "I answered yes. I want to stay." He replied, "It is not your time to remain here."

Elizabeth said she wanted to stay there so badly but the male spirit asked her about her children and told Elizabeth she had to go back to them but some day she would return. He said, "There is more for you to do in your physical experience." Elizabeth begged to stay and as she was doing this she began to float away from the light. Very quickly she found herself back in her body. The physicians in the surgical suite looked at her and said, "Welcome back." The doctors who had performed the surgery knew she had died on the table and had returned.

Elizabeth says she will always remember this experience. It was a gift because she will never fear death. She said to me, "When one gets rid of the death card, there's only life. The light is real. Live your soul's life. I am grateful for this experience because it's allowed me to be free. During the experience I felt love pulling me."

The happy ending to this story is that Elizabeth became healthy and raised her children. Looking back she is grateful she was able to come back to her husband and children as she loves them so much. She never told the doctors what happened to her on the operating table. For her, this has been a life-changing event and she wants all of us to know that death is not an end, but instead a beginning.

Postscript

Elizabeth is guided by the Archangel Gabriel and so she reached out to this Angel to help her validate or confirm which spirits she spoke to during her near-death experience.

She began to write spontaneously as she listened to his words. She wrote this about the female spirit, "It was I, the Mother of whom was to come! We love you and are always with you! Remember us in prayer! Stay on the road simply as you are." Elizabeth felt this was the Virgin Mother Mary. She continued to write about the male figure. "I am called Jesus, Savior, and Messiah. We love you! This will help you return from whence you came. We honor you and we are always with you. Share these words as your soul commands. You are the life, and you are living for others and we are very pleased. As you continue in this life we bless you and ask you to do the same for others. From your blessings will come great healings?" It was very clear to Elizabeth after this channeled message she had been guided

46

by Jesus and Mary. *I thank Elizabeth for sharing her lovely story with all of us.*

Lingering Death

"I am not a body. I am free. I am as God created me."
The Course in Miracles

I asked Saint Germain to help me understand a slow death with physical suffering? Saint Germain said, "The choice of suffering is chosen in order to resolve past conflict. For instance, one might be atoning for a killing on the battlefield and have chosen physical incapacitation for this purpose. There is a reason for all choices. As you know, most aspects of one's living and dying are pre-planned and considered carefully by one's guides and teachers."

I asked if the place of death was important. He said, "It is part of one's decision and choice as to how to die." I asked him specifically about my brother. He went to college in the same town where he died. He began as a college student in this town and 35 years later died from a drug over dose in the same area. Saint Germain said we choose the place to leave the earth. It is part of our decision. He continued to say, "Your brother knew he would leave his body in this significant place. It represents the life he rejected, the life he loved, and the life he was ready to move on from." I continued to pursue this topic by asking, "What do you mean by rejected?" Saint Germain replied, "Your brother did not make the decision to attend college; others made it for him, therefore it was a choice he rejected?" This stunned me. My parents expected all of us to attend college. They never asked us if we wanted this academic experience. I asked for clarification about the comment, "*the life he loved.*" Saint Germain said my brother was able to assist others and at the same time he lost himself. His final action was to leave in his own way and in doing so he helped his own soul.

I asked Saint Germain about dying as a drug user. He said, "When one is unconsciousness from the intervention of unnecessary drugs the experience of dying is spoiled. Dying is a glorious and uplifting experience. This cloud, from the use of unnecessary drugs is quickly removed upon arrival, but it is still a block to having had the full experience of dying."

What will the angels ask us when we die? He said, they will embrace you and say, "Do you understand you have left your physical body? What have you learned and who have you helped? This is the first question followed by, you are safe, and we will help you find your loved ones and a place to rest." The most important words in this paragraph are underlined. They are at the core of why we came into a physical body in the first place.

I wondered what happens in the grave. Saint Germain said there is nothing in the grave except the shell of a physical body. I asked him, "Why is burial so popular?" He answered, "It is the belief the body is who you are, and the body must be retained in some fashion; placed in the earth and marked. You are not a body, you are a force. You are created in the image of God."

"Why do some people see angels when they cross over to the other side and others don't?" He answered, "Each birth and death is unique. There are some souls who require more assistance prior to the journey and the angels are there to reassure them all is well. Others are ready to leave their bodies and will join these heavenly companions immediately upon departure."

"Do most souls leave in happiness or in sorrow?" Saint Germain answered, "Both. Many are afraid to leave souls who still rely on them for care. Souls who have released their earthly responsibilities and obligations take this very brief journey feeling great relief and comfort. We work hard with those who are still looking back with a sense of worry regarding their loved ones. They are reassured all is well and their spiritual teams work behind the material plane to assist and comfort them."

"I have to ask this important question about the fear of losing the breath. Breathing is so natural to us. The thought of its cessation can actually bring up the topic of suffocation." He responded, "The loss of one's breath is part of the dying process that disturbs many. The departure from the body is so rapid. One takes a last breath in the body and begins another here." So I responded, do we breathe? He said, "Yes for a few moments. There is no need for the breath. After the journey one will feel as if the breath continues. Its absence is hardly noticed. Eventually, you will realize the astral body is lighter and has no need of oxygen." He asked me, "Do you focus your attention on your breath now?" I answered, "Yes, when I am meditating, running or anxious." He repeated again, "It is of no importance and once you experience this again you will fully understand it."

"Do some people have difficulty understanding they've

actually made the crossing to the other side?" Saint Germain said, "Yes. Many are very surprised to learn they no longer inhabit a physical body; even as they see their loved ones standing behind the curtain. We assist each soul at the level of their own understanding. Each requires a unique approach. One who takes his or her own life is assisted differently than an elderly gentleman who died as he slept. All is intimately and intricately managed by those trained to guide the soul to the next event and the continuing life."

Sudden Death

"But at the time of transition, your guides your guardian angels, people whom you have loved and who have passed on before you, will be there to help you. We have verified this beyond a shadow of a doubt, and I say this as a scientist. There will always be someone to help you with this transition." Elizabeth Kubler-Ross

I asked about a sudden death which occurred in Ohio. There was a teenager riding an amusement park ride and one of the cars became damaged and flew off the ride's main support. It was in our newspapers and very upsetting. I asked, "What was the experience like for the boy?" Saint Germain said they were aware of the accident and the guardian angel and Chief Elder knew there were probabilities associated with this moment. One probability would be the death of an individual. He said, "The soul's angelic team was ready to respond." It was unclear what he meant by probabilities but Saint Germain continued to say this, "It is the responsibility of the guides and angels to always be on watch. If you were facing a potential life altering event ahead of your time I would be notified immediately, but the smaller events are monitored by the angels."

I wondered about the consequences of an unsuccessful transition? "Once I read a successful transition allows all the parts of our previous experience to continue to function together after the body is let go. I am not sure I understand this?" Saint Germain liked the question and said, "Yes, one must retain the memories of your life. Any condition removing memories prior to death will cause a partial transition. However, your memories are returned to you after your arrival here. They are scattered and souls who work on the first platform collect the pieces and re-integrate the memories." So I asked, "When we arrive on the other side are we aware we crossed over without our full mental capacity?" He responded, "Yes."

The answer to the previous question implies we could lose memories? I wondered if an unsuccessful transition means all pieces fall apart and our experiences are left hanging in some way; like somebody who is emotionally disturbed and cannot connect the pieces of their life. He replied, "No, however, for someone who is emotionally disabled, the pieces are integrated over a period of time."

"Do we carry all our negative experiences into the afterlife?" Saint Germain said, "Yes, one carries all the baggage." "What about accidents; especially when it involves young people or a baby who becomes very ill?" He said, "A young child is handled carefully and is given the memories of the previous life leading up to an early death. Many decisions are made based upon the ability of the soul to understand what has happened. Frequently old souls leave as infants in order to help their families learn a particular lesson."

I commented, "The Master Hilarion said people with a weak life force will lose part of their higher selves in death. Does this mean that we could be transferred to another soul group; for instance an animal soul group?" He said yes, "this is considered a great loss."

Saint Germain says it is very sad for souls who fail to function in a physical body. There may be evil and wrong doing towards others. These souls may lose the life force or be returned to the universal substance. There is a penalty for people who do terrible things. I reminded him we had spoken about this before in reference to the terrible shooting in Las Vegas in 2017. This took the lives of at least 60 souls. I reminded him of an earlier conversation when he told me a soul could be returned to this universal pool of substance and it is considered a sad event when it happens. He said, "Yes, this is very sad as we mourn the loss of each precious life."

I asked if a soul can be lost forever when there is an estrangement between the soul and the personality. Saint Germain said "Yes, a soul can die; but a better way to express this is to say a soul can be assimilated. No soul substance is lost. This is a decision made carefully and infrequently." Saint Germain continued to say there is a universal pool of substance from which souls are created. There are souls who are returned to the original substance from where they were born. This only pertains to souls who have committed evil deeds and cannot be saved, or for those who request to die permanently. I was surprised to learn somebody could request a permanent death, and he answered me by saying this, "Yes indeed, however, it is rare and only chosen as a last resort for those who have, after great care and rehabilitation, given up and made the request. This is the gift of your own free will."

Is there a tunnel created by souls welcoming the person who has died? Saint Germain said, "Yes, there is a vortex of energy as you are embraced by souls who await your return. A group of souls are called and the tunnel is a creation of the light formed by the gathering. The soul, who is transported to a new life, is also a light being and adds to the presence of this tunnel."

One day, I was running late between appointments and I had not eaten. I stopped at a restaurant for breakfast. A gentleman sat down next to me at the counter. He didn't know who I was but he began to share his near death story. He said, "I have had three brain operations and I almost died during the last one. I was tempted to go. I saw a light and there were hundreds of hands beckoning me to come." He continued to say, all he could see were hands. I loved this little conversation and I said to him, "I want you to know the hands are part of the tunnel of light." We ended our conversation by his saying, "I thought so." The important thing to know is this tunnel of light you hear about in near-death experiences is created by souls coming to greet us, and of course, they will be beckoning us with what appears to be their hands.

"Is there such a thing as an unsuccessful crossing?" Saint Germain said, "Yes, this is true for those who forget the demise of the human body. (Meaning souls unaware they have died). There are guides who work to create an easy transition but there are younger souls who hold onto the fabric of physicality; particularly souls who possess all the material desires but no real understanding of their relationship to others and purpose for being human." I asked him to expound on this by asking how the transition is unsuccessful. He said, "There are souls caught between the lower vibrations of the planet and the higher dimensions of spirit. They are left in a state of limbo until they are convinced to move on or to give up."

My next question was, "What is it like for a criminal who is put to death by lethal injection?" Saint Germain said, "It is an instant death. The spiritual team assists the soul to a place of love and rehabilitation. There is a process in which these souls re-deem themselves. The soul is counseled by those prepared to unravel the reasons for criminal behavior, and following rehabilitation they are introduced again to the light."

Dying Consciously

"There are only two faces to existence — birth and death, and life survives them both. Just as sunrise and sunset are not essentially different: it all depends on whether one is facing east or west." Joy Mills

I asked Saint Germain if we can be fully conscious when we pass through the dying process. I mentioned some of the great Indian Masters who were able to die consciously. "Can anybody do this?" He answered me saying, "There are those souls who through deep meditation are already *in a soul sense* here within the higher vibrations. So you see, for a soul like this, it is simply a process of cutting the cord. This is done within a deep state of meditation, and is allowed when a soul has been given permission to choose their own date of death, and needs no assistance to make the journey. The one to whom you refer was a master and he walked in and out of the place you call heaven. He needed no key. It was his responsibility to serve many, therefore his situation was special."

I asked if this was also the same for Jesus. "Did he choose to leave before his body died on the cross?" Saint Germain answered "Yes." I mentioned reading about a technique of dying by focusing on the third eye. There are some who just simply withdraw their consciousness as if they're going to sleep and it stays intact as they cross over to the astral plane. Is there such a thing? Saint Germain said, "Yes, you are delving into the deeper mysteries now. There is a technique where one focus's on the area between the eyebrows: the third eye. Then one withdraws consciousness to the head to keep contact with the astral plane. They see themselves in a waiting area; one waits within this space outside the gate. This is the entrance- the door between life and death."

He went on to say, "Being conscious through the death process is the best way to die. In order to do this you must be alert. Some souls are not conscious until they arrive on the other side; some die under sedation making conscious dying difficult."

"It is said when a liberated spiritual man dies he or she blends in with the *over soul* on the higher levels of the mental plane. Can you explain the *over soul?*" Saint Germain said "Yes, it is the totality of who you are; the sum of all life experiences within bodies. There will be an integration of the memories but these memories are handled by your Council. You are given these memories slowly based upon your ability to re-integrate them. Some souls do not see the whole; only the parts."

A Personal Story

"Death is only an interlude in a life of accumulating experience. It marks a definite transition from one state of consciousness into another."

John Halliwell

Born April 7, 1927 —Died, December 20, 2003.

This man was my father, He died of stomach cancer. He was afraid of dying. He was born with a life path number of three which means it was important for him to speak his truth. He was a good and honest soul. He left the physical life on a number one signaling accomplishment. Close to the end of his life I said, "Daddy, are you afraid to die?" He responded, "Do you think I am going to die Jane?" He did not want to leave.

He was the best man I ever knew with the exception of my husband Don. He was self -less. He was instrumental in raising the funds to build a beautiful library in his town of Camp Hill, Pennsylvania. There is a statue dedicated to him in this community. He loved reading and is responsible for my love of books.

I have had very little contact with him from the other side, but every time I do hear from him it is a warning to be careful. About 12 years ago I was scheduled to give a presentation in Brunswick, Maine. I was living in Portland, Maine at the time. The night before my presentation I had a dream and my father told me to stay on the right side of the road avoiding the passing lane. As I was leaving Brunswick and driving in the passing lane, an oversized tractor trailer was barreling down the road behind me. I quickly remembered his warning and moved to the right lane before the truck rear-ended my car. I believe my father saved my life that day. So messages from the other side will arrive in many ways. Always pay attention to them.

This is my conversation with him facilitated by Saint Germain"

When I began this conversation I saw Saint Germain come forward along with Jesus. Jesus said to me, "Your father was a good man. He was not a young soul. He always placed others before himself." I responded, "He was not religious however?" Jesus replied, "Yes, he was raised in a house without religion in order to see a different viewpoint. His marriage to your mother helped him to re- connect with the loss of faith; to reclaim what was his prior to the life as John."

All souls choose lives for the experience. A student in college might ponder, "What class will contribute to my growth, or add to my resume of job skills."

I now spoke directly to my father and said, daddy, you look younger than me!

"I've learned age is very unimportant."

Is mom with you?

"Yes she is with me now. We are having fun traveling to all of our favorite places."

How's the food in France? (I *knew this was his favorite place!).*

"It satisfies the need to remember the prior experience. It's not the same but fairly decent."

I asked him if he knew about my work as a spiritual medium.

He said he has watched Saint Germain work with me from the other side. I found this fascinating.

Did you attend your own funeral?

"Yes, in my sleep. I don't know how long I slept but it felt like a long time. I was woken up and I felt a little confused. My guides reminded me that I was dead and I felt very disoriented."

Are you aware of family members back here on earth? Have your guides allowed you to look in on us?

"Yes, I have been offered this, but I am afraid to look. It causes me heartache when I see the kids and can't help them. I decided to wait until they come here."
(I found this very interesting---and typical of my father to avoid looking if he couldn't actively help.)

I mentioned his grandson who has become very

successful as a golfer. I asked him if he would like to know how he is doing.

"I've heard all about Peter from your mother. We talked about all the grandchildren. I knew Peter would be a great athlete." (*My mother joined him in 2016*).

Have you talked to Brother John?
(*My brother was a drug addict and crossed over in 2015*).

"Yes, we are together all the time. We've worked with the Elders to resolve our past difficulties. I understand John now and see how our family was created. The choices were made carefully."

What is your favorite activity?

"Travel to southern France. I have had many lifetimes in this country."

I'm writing a book about death. What would you like everyone to know about heaven?

"It's another great experience; another steppingstone. I wasn't sure if anything existed after death but I found out quickly I was wrong. It was a relief to realize life goes on. I cried. No tears but complete relief and then I slept."

I closed the conversation by telling him I missed him. He responded that he feels my emotions whenever I think of him.

This is why it's so important for us to always telepathically communicate with our loved ones who have crossed over! They hear us!!!

I asked if he had anything he wanted to say to my sisters who are here still living.

"Tell them I love them and I am waiting to see you all. I'll be at the gate ready to hold you in my arms. I'll be your special tour guide here in heaven."

5 REST AND REUNION WITH LOVED ONES

"The reality of my life cannot die, for I am indestructible consciousness."
Paramahansa Yogananda

When we arrive on the other side we sleep. This is not a choice. Saint Germain says, "Each soul rests in a place similar to your hotels. Some rest for many years of your earth time, others have short naps because they know the terrain here. Each soul is unique and is treated as an individual. We consider the circumstances of the death in serving each soul.

The life review

I asked Saint Germain to describe the life review. He says the following "The life review is managed by one's Council of Elders and the majority of souls experience this after greeting close family members, friends, and spent time sleeping. Once one has been awakened; and this is not sleep in the sense you understand it while in a body; the soul sits quietly with their Council of Elders."

"The review begins with a summary of all key events of the last physical life. The highlights of the life are given special importance. Each council member is responsible for a certain number of years. The lifespan is generally divided into as many pieces as the size of the Council. I asked him if that meant for somebody who lived to 100 and had five council members each one would discuss 20 years of the life. He said, "Yes, and went on to say, there is a complete discussion of each segment of the life. Questions are asked of you, such as what do you remember about this particular event? How could this have been handled differently? The returning soul is given the opportunity to sum up the years of the life as simply as possible. The Council asks you to grade yourself. They also ask how you would improve upon that grade."

I asked if the life is projected in front of the Council and the returning soul like a movie. He responded, "It depends on the individual soul. There are younger souls who require a return to the scene, and for them it is played as a movie."

I asked, "What happens next?" He said, "One is asked to choose a school and a task; a project if you will; in order to prepare for the next experience within a human body."

I asked what he meant by tasks, or the responsibilities souls take on. He said this, "For a very young soul there will be time spent in re-enacting events; seeing the results of an action from a previous life differently. This is like a movie set, but one plays the actions back. Some souls re-visit a life event hundreds of times; others are able to release the karma in one or two re-turns. (*Karma means past actions*).

I asked a personal question about myself, "What will this life review look like for me?" He said I will be asked for my preferences and I will be able to select the life events I found difficult. He said, "You will lift them up to a higher

62

level quickly.

I asked Saint Germain how they recognize a soul. He laughed at me and said, "It is seen as a unique energy. Just as each person has a unique face and voice, the soul is the same. It is original, with special attributes given to it upon birth. You will understand when you experience it. All families and past generations are united. Your guides notify your family that you are arriving moments prior to your crossing. It is easy to re-connect with your elders and families.

Souls gather together in a spirit of celebration. There is always a reunion with our loved ones!

Saint Germain says we will see our loved ones as souls, not bodies... He says, "Your friends and family must meet you at the soul level. This is both in your physical lives and on the other side." He continues to say, "The soul is energy and can be easily recognized. While in bodies we fail to see the most important part of another person which is their soul. On earth your soul is quietly disguised."

He went on to say, we all have something called an *auric echo* which is like a birthmark. He continued to say, "We are able to see and feel the echo of all souls. The echo is also experienced when leaving the human body behind. He said, "The soul is identified by the echo. It is difficult to hear it from the physical plane but many; particularly old souls pick up the energy." I asked Saint Germain if this echo is like the high-pitched tone I sometimes hear when I am channeling. He said, "No, it is a deeper tone and is unique to the soul.

Once you identify the auric echo, you will always hear it in the same way. Just as you are unique because of your physical characteristics, so is the auric echo unique. The high-pitched tone you hear is connection to a very high vibration beyond your earthly environment.

Mental Telepathy

In heaven we communicate by using mental telepathy. Mind to mind communication is perfectly natural for us. Mental telepathy is very simply communication without the five senses. I said, "What if we are all talking at the same time?" Saint Germain laughed and said, "Within a permeable light body a thought is never missed. However, in your physical environment thoughts are almost always missed." Just think how amazing this is. Our thoughts are so powerful and think of how many we miss!!

Saint Germain said we should experiment by transmitting thoughts to others while living in our physical bodies. He said, "Those individuals who can send a thought to another soul and know they have received a response, qualifiy as an old soul." So, there is a common language on the other side.

Saint Germain wants us to work on our telepathic ability now. He says this, "See the world as a bowl of soup filled with information ready to be sipped. You have the ability within you to receive these hidden messages." If we can master non-verbal human communication while we are in our physical bodies, then we can also hear the unspoken thoughts of our loved ones. He says, "It's important for us to know that every time we think of our loved ones who have crossed over they pick up our thoughts." He says, "One must first believe the loved ones are receptive to your thoughts and love. Know, as you think of your mother and father here they feel the energy and love of your thoughts. Sending and receiving thoughts is not simply relegated to the physical earth. All your thoughts and feelings are felt by those in spiritual bodies. They know, and are blessed each time you send them love and memories of your time together. Take a moment in the morning and evening to speak to them. Know they receive your messages."

We actually communicate by telepathy. Saint Germain says there is no common language. Communication is by thought, or if desired, the spoken word. If someone had recently left a particular country in which a certain tongue was spoken, they might speak to those who carry the same memory of the language but most will choose to communicate by thought transference. I returned to the question of the breath and said, "Isn't the breath necessary in order to speak? " He said, "No, it can be done without the breath and very nicely." He said I would remember instantly when I returned to spirit because all skills of maneuvering and managing in that environment come back instantly.

Do we sleep when we first arrive?

He said, "This decision varies widely between souls. It is your choice. One meets loved ones and the Council member responsible for the entry details. You will discuss the details of your arrival and your rest. Once one is asleep it is natural for the soul to awake when ready. Some sleep for many months of earth time, others only for a few hours, and some for only a period of days."

When we arrive on the other side we are allowed to meet our families. I wanted to know how far back the reunion with former family members goes. I was told our true family line is not based upon birth and a lineage associated with the last family. Family lineage is the entire line of loved ones we are associated with. Our body represents many genetic heritages. In spirit we will seek out and reunite with loved ones from centuries ago including many family lines.

I asked him about sleep. "Is there a need for sleep?" He said, "There is no need to sleep. The spiritual body is a light body unencumbered by physical needs." He also added "there is no need to eat, rest, or even speak." He went on to say, "You will be thrilled to be free of the requirement to rest because you will be very productive."

Can we see the full moon on the other side?

Saint Germain was amused by my question. "Yes, you will see planetary bodies. Spirit envelops all the physical worlds. You will find an area of the cosmos most interesting and familiar to you as souls instinctively remember how to see in this way."

I asked if other planetary systems can be seen. For instance, if I came from another place would I see my planetary home?

"Yes, however, it is a decision the elders will help you to make. It is important that all aspects of the life just lived are addressed immediately. Later, one can visit other homes in the universe."

Can we see Earth?

"Yes, it is possible but very few request this. Once one leaves of earth there is no desire to look back."

Science says the Universe has no end. How would you describe it?

Saint Germain answered, "This is true. The universe does not end and is constantly expanding. To say more would be beyond your ability to comprehend."

Do we dream on the other side?

"Yes, of course! He reminded me we are not in our body when we dream; he said the same thing happens when we are in our deeper consciousness following death. Dreams provide us with lessons and symbols of what lies ahead and this information continues to flow on the other side. Dreaming is encouraged when we arrive, but later, it is discouraged as souls begin to plan for a return to a human body.

Saint Germain continues to say, "You dream as you

choose to sleep. There is no need to sleep. Instead, these are choices. One dreams of their own funeral and family gathering during sleep. Physical death is only one side of the equation. Spiritual life is the other side. Dreaming is a past-time loved by many souls."

I commented, "It seems as if there are many choices and some fall into the category of recreation?" He said, "this is true, and for some souls it is rest and for others simply a way to escape the duties on the other side. Over time, dreams become unnecessary. Dreams are more important to humans limited by their physical bodies. Dreams expand their consciousness and provide a connection to us here. Once you have arrived in the non-physical realms it is unnecessary for the spiritual body to sleep or to dream."

What responsibilities do we have on the other side?

Saint Germain said, "You choose an area of interest. Some work with young souls who are in early lives; others assist souls in the Hall of Records. Some receive souls upon their journey home; others work with the elders or souls who are choosing new lives. This is a busy place filled with love, light, and an enthusiasm missing from the earth where energies can be denser."

The Hall of Records is the location in heaven where the history of all our lifetimes (the Akashic Records) is stored.

If somebody dies living on another planet, what are the differences between this other world and earth?

"The differences are minor. Those who await the

arrival of souls from Earth resemble them physically in appearance and this is true for other planetary systems. When one arrives here there is a rapid return to a light body which is not gender or origination specific."

We see those who greet us in bodies displaying familiar characteristics'.

"You will release the memory of the unique physical body very quickly. You relate to each other as souls not bodies. The old ones (*souls who have had numerous lives*) have had outer planet experiences and quickly adjust."

I understand there are different planes in the spiritual world occupying the same space and with different frequencies? When I am living on earth there are spiritual aspects of me reflected on the spiritual plane? These planes are all at a different frequency similar to radio. The vibrations occupy the same space at the same time but different channels. Because they are on different frequencies they do not collide.

Saint Germain replied, "Yes, there is a deep sound in the upper frequencies. There are levels like the stations on your radio. You can become aware of these energies as they resonate in sound. Older souls tune into the higher frequencies, younger souls do not."

How do we distinguish between the two?

"I have not taught you this yet. You are aware of the other frequencies, and each day you walk in and out of the energy of many." I asked him if this happens during meditation, He replied, "Yes, in meditation you are floating between two or three frequencies and when one goes deeper into meditation you reach the higher energies where I myself reside. So, if you are attuned to this message you will be aware of going in and out of these energies. When we work together you transcend human frequencies to reach into the space from where I speak. You are here in your soul, not body."

When we think of our loved ones, do they know we are thinking about them? If the loved one just popped into our head, does this mean they are thinking about us?

"Yes, this is possible, and you may be remembering them also. Memories are often triggered by an object which belongs to a loved one."

Do we celebrate holidays on the other side?

"No, not in the way one celebrates while in the body. There are celebrations here, however these are soul gatherings and opportunities to share love between yourself and others. For instance, one celebrates an initiate moving to a higher classroom."

Do souls get a tour of the terrain?

"Yes, it is not difficult to maneuver here as one's thoughts create the energy to transition between the layers of heaven. A soul is given personal instruction by their guides. This is the most important relationship upon one's arrival here."

Is the life review experience like a cleansing?

"No, however one would call this a deep reflection into all aspects of the previous life; including a complete and very thorough discussion with the elders. There are many aspects of your life as a soul, you have forgotten. All experiences are revealed and the elders create a plan for your time in spirit. This is an educational plan."

In the Life Review are our thoughts as important as our actions? If someone thought about stealing a car but did not act on those thoughts, how does the Council treat this? After all our thoughts control our behavior?

Saint Germain said, "Your thoughts matter at all times; even when you have not acted upon the thought. Thoughts are energy and represent your soul's behavior. In other words, they are indicative of your inclinations and your possible actions."

In my readings I see souls who have chosen to continue surrounding themselves with a physical experience on the other side. These are usually younger souls. They still eat and live in some type of house. When they appear in a reading, I notice they are dressed in clothes reminiscent of the time period they died. I have also seen souls who are choosing to stay on non- physical layers in heaven. They wear robes of different colors, teach, and help souls at the lower levels. Can you tell me what the nonphysical experience is like for souls?

Saint Germain said, "The souls who reside in the upper layers work diligently to bring the others upward – to the next grade you see. It is the goal to use this time between lives to elevate souls in preparation for the next life. Those in the robes are spiritual teachers and they rotate responsibilities."

Is it required for all souls to return to a physical body?

Saint Germain said, "Yes, for souls who have not earned ascension it is required. We do not choose the time, but encourage the soul to move ahead – not to linger here when work needs to be accomplished."

We have the gift of free will. Our teachers on the other side will encourage us to return to a body when the time is right; however, we have free will and can decide to stay in the spiritual world longer.

Are there hot and cold sensations?

"Yes, they are created by your mind. The sensations are created from your memories. I remind you, your mind and thoughts are powerful."

Is there a sun and do we feel the heat?

"Yes, the mind will create exactly what it desires to see and feel. " I continued to ask, "Since we do not have bodies how can we feel anything?" Saint Germain said, "You have bodies. They are not as dense as physical flesh and bone but nonetheless one can feel and move these vehicles quickly and smoothly in order to travel amongst the world's here."

Is there a place to live?

He laughed when I asked this question and said, "Yes, you create it from your memories." I asked if it would be as real as a place I love on the earth. He said "yes, you will choose a place in Ireland. As you reside here in these higher vibrations you also connect with the physical aspects of the land of Ireland. The higher vibrations are superimposed on dense physical matter so your experience in Ireland is closely related to your physical preferences however, the energetic vibration is higher.
Yes, many choose to re-build the last residence. Some choose to be in a place known and loved in the physical life." He went on to say we move by thought instantly.

It sounds like we find what we expect. Is this true? Seventh-day Adventists believe they will sleep until Jesus comes again. Is this what they will experience?

"Yes, this will be their experience but they are quickly told the truth. Jesus does not return, as he is always present. It is understood when guides share this information."

Do our surrounding seen real or dreamlike?

"They will feel real in every respect. You will change the environment based on your desires. Nothing here is heavy or requires physical strength to change. It is a creation of your own memories and the place you create will appear very solid and real to you." He continued to say, "Your surroundings look solid; as solid as the desk you write upon. It is your creation. Is it not? Understand this; all thoughts become matter and one's creations appear very solid here."

How far back can we go in order to meet loved ones in our family line?

"The ancestral line is endless. You will see those who have many connections with your soul. You will see the records of all your relationships and be given the opportunity to meet with these souls. It is the long-term relationship you will treasure, not the ones of brevity."
In other words, we will relate to people that we've loved and had a significant amount of time with; not necessarily the line of relatives on our genetic trail.

What physical being are we all related to? Was it Adam and Eve? Was it Noah or was it Darwin's evolution theory? Who were the first souls responsible for the human race? Where on earth did they originate?

"You are not related to any physical being. Your soul begins as pure soul energy; to be imprinted by yourself through experience. Evolution of the species is facilitated by us. It is not completely natural. It can be pushed ahead to move faster. In the original plan there were masters designing and manipulating matter into physical form."

How is grief handled?

"It is easy. The soul who arrives here is home. The world of form is not your natural home. Just as you have loved souls on the physical plane, you will embrace those who died previously. You are shown the support provided to loved ones who were left behind on earth. There is rapid relief."

What does the first platform look like when we arrive? Does it resemble a city, classroom, or hospital setting? My husband Don had a past life regression and saw a city. The area outside the city was dark?

"It resembles your beliefs. You will see Ireland and the ocean. Another soul will create a place of comfort familiar to them. The vision is individual."

Where is the afterlife? Explain the overlap of the vibrations?

"It is everywhere; in and around all physical matter. The subtle energies are integrated with the dense physical substance. There are those who accidentally stumble upon it. Many see it during their dreams. You are here often and to do so you must override the dense energy and travel in your light body to study with us."

In a second channeled session he said, "It is everywhere you look and envelops all physical worlds. It is the matrix holding all other physical spheres together. You may use glue as the best metaphor. Glue is often colorless is it not?" I answered, "Yes." He continued to say, "The higher vibrations are binding; energetically tough and resilient. We are very close to each other. The vibration is higher here, but as you vibrate at a higher level you move closer to me."

I have spoken to Saint Germain many times about this question. The afterlife is so close some of us can hear a high-pitched sound; usually in one ear. This sound is the higher tone or vibration of the afterlife.

When you hear this tone, it is an indication you are an old soul. When a spiritual medium channels, she or he must reach upward to connect with this subtle field of energy; In doing so there is a connection with the Master Teacher, or guide.

Why has it taken so long for us to become spiritually perfect? Some of us have lived thousands of lives, and still do not get it. At what point can we be given permanent status in the spiritual world?

"It is up to you. You can achieve perfection in five lifetimes or 500. The soul decides, and the Council of Elders monitors the progress."

I need some advice for family members left behind. Is it true the one who has died can look back at their family but the reverse doesn't happen?

"Yes, this is true. "The one who has returned home can begin a new life. Looking backwards is not encouraged, however some do. Those in physical bodies are assisted by guides. There is no value in chasing a soul who has risen."
Saint Germain refers to a soul who has died.
"This is because there is no separation, except what you refer to as death. Souls always re-unite."

Where does a really bad person go when they die?

"There are many groups constantly forming and holding needy souls close. There is a well-organized plan for those needing re-education, just as for those who have ascended to the light."

Do we forget our families?

"No, never. All relationships are remembered by the soul. One moves into relationships regardless of historical time markers. You connect with souls regardless of the years of physical separation."

Is there a healing center on the other side?

"Yes, there are many centers. They are constantly receiving souls. All souls pass through a gate and into other arenas. There are souls who linger as they do not understand what has occurred to bring them home. Others understand where they are immediately and are escorted to the areas where greetings and celebrations are being held. Those who come here suddenly through accident or long illness remain in the healing centers the longest."

What about suicide? Is it treated as an accident?

"It is not treated as an accident. The soul makes the decision and it is serious use of one's free will. Elders work with these souls to determine the reasons for the action of killing one's body."

Does death feel like a dream or is it very real?

"It is often felt like a dream for one who transitions in sleep or severe illness. Those who cross quickly are immediately aware of everything. They are in an open and responsive state. There can be a moment of hesitation and the dreamlike quality fades quickly. Life here is very real and we have an active and thriving community."

Can someone on the other side make someone here who is in a body see them?

I mentioned my vision of St. Padre Pio and Saint Germain. This happened to me in the middle of the night. I woke up, sat up in bed and saw two figures clearly standing at the bottom of my bed. Saint Germain said to me, "We lowered our vibration and heightened yours. We met in the middle."

Do we travel on the other side?   And if we do, will we see souls who are still in bodies as well as souls out of bodies, or just spiritual bodies like ourselves?

Saint Germain has a sense of humor and he had a little chuckle at my expense. He said he had seen the question in my mind!   He said, "You will see all souls; however there is a difference between those in bodies and those in spirit. Those who are embodied will only see those like themselves."

I thought this was interesting. When we travel we see both earthbound and spiritual beings but earth-based humans cannot see us. I asked him if we would bump into and hear these embodied souls. He said no, "You will glide through them.   They cannot hear you and you cannot obstruct their growth. You must simply enjoy the place. It is common for souls to re-visit places they have loved. You will meet and enjoy souls who have died, like you, and are visiting this particular place."   I responded, "So you say we see souls like ourselves – in lighter vehicles/spiritual bodies? Saint Germain responded by saying, "There are accidents when one does bump into matter but this is unusual." This last sentence made me pause and I asked him another question, "How can a spiritual body run up against a dense body?" He answered my question by saying this, "There are some souls who may feel the spiritual body of one here in the higher vibrations. The connection must be direct in that one must move physically against the spirit. The soul within the dense human body rarely notices this. Sensitives might feel the presence or feel something touching them, but dismiss this as imagination."

I asked if I could drink a glass of wine or a beer on the other side.

He said, "Yes, if you choose. It is not the same but very good."

Do we retain our gender?

"You retain your gender for as long as you like. It is your decision. Most souls never release the gender and some do immediately. There are some who take on the gender which was comfortable for them in other lives. Souls will choose a light body they loved from past incarnations. Most souls retain the previous body's characteristics."

Are there celebrations on the other side?

"There are many events; too many to name. When souls graduate from one level to another friends and family gather. When Masters come to teach there is a gathering in celebration. Upon the arrival of loved ones, there is often merriment, rejoicing and celebration. Each moment here is a new experience consisting of uplifting energy. Even those who struggle to overcome the past are drawn into the light of souls gathering in joy.

Are there celebrations to say goodbye to those leaving the spirit world, or does the life on earth happen so fast they barely miss us?

"This is very personal. Most souls leave this higher energy with their Elders by their side. It is a sacred journey and there is a ritual I cannot share with you."

Is there a hell?

"No, not in the way it is depicted on earth. Hell here is the struggle to overcome past mistakes and the task of re-visiting each event. All attempts to remember past memories are carefully guarded and monitored by the angels and guides assigned to you. The worst that can happen is a soul will be returned to the universal pool of substance."

I don't understand the need to transform from pure soul energy to a physical body containing a soul? Couldn't we learn, experience all the lessons in the spiritual world as we could in a physical form?

"One learns lessons in physical matter. There are consequences for one's actions. Living in a physical body on a planetary body with dense energy is the greatest school in the universe. Here, in the higher vibrations one's thoughts are instantly manifested, and therefore the lessons are easy. One grows faster in a dense physical body."

In the spirit world, it is all unconditional love. Why is it necessary to experience hate, anger, resentment, anxiety, and failure in the physical form? What are we being prepared for? It almost seems like we are being punished. What is wrong with a world of unconditional love that needs to be changed or improved?

"To grow! It would take much longer to reach ascension and the higher platforms here without the experience in a physical body. One learns unconditional love through adversity and struggle."

A Personal Story

"If the body is a lightbulb, and it burns out, does that mean there is no more electricity? The source of energy remains." Joseph Campbell

Edmund S.

I knew this individual for a very short time; however, he made a significant difference in my life. It is said that some people come into our lives for a moment, a season, or a lifetime. Edmund came into my life for a moment and for a reason. I learned three years after meeting him and saying good-bye he had died. I knew when I met him he was a very old soul. He had read the Course in Miracles so many times he was on his fourth hard bound book. I knew what an amazing feat that was. Saint Germain told me we had known each other in many lifetimes. I wanted to find out what his experience of death was.

Saint Germain said Edmund did not take good care of his body. He said, "It was not important to him and he was anxious to move on." I asked, "Did he die consciously?" Saint Germain said, "Yes, he died quickly and asked to be removed from his body. Many came to his bedside. He was a candidate for Ascension and he has entered a special portal for Ascension candidates. He was happy to be there."

Ascension - means a soul does not need to come back into a physical body ever again.

This is my conversation with Edmund.
He died at the age of 72. He was an amazing oil painter and

shared my love of the country of Ireland. This interview is a good example of an older soul crossing over to the other side.

Were you ill when I met you for the first time?

"I was not ill at that time, but I was not feeling good. I met you just before I was diagnosed with a heart condition."

Did you fight this illness?

"I was anxious to stay in my physical body. I put up a good fight, but I knew in the last year of my life I was going to move on." *He laughed as he said this.*

Can you tell me what you remember when you crossed over?

"Yes, I remember every part of this experience. It was beautiful. I stayed awake. I saw angels in my room and they surrounded me with their light and lifted me up higher and higher. It was a wonderful feeling of floating. Then I sat up in bed and realized I was in a hospital but not the same room. Saint Germain was there and a guide named Emell. I asked if I had arrived in heaven and everyone laughed and hugged me. I was relieved. I thought to myself, I made it across the line!"

What did you do next?

"I rested and then was shown the territory."

Explain what this territory looks like to you?

"The area is massive; like being in Ireland and seeing miles of fields stretching ahead. It was breathtaking; and I felt total peace. I knew I was home. I experienced complete relaxation and comfort."

Did you have an opportunity to sleep again?

"No, I was allowed to rest when I chose to rest. There was too much to see and I was spending time with Saint Germain learning the next steps. I am staying here this time and will work on behalf of others as a spiritual guide."
He was told he could remain in heaven and never re-incarnate into a body again.

Have you seen your family back on earth?

"Yes. I know they are okay. I am not concerned with them now because I understand the amazing support given to those left behind. What was invisible to me in a human body, I can see clearly now."

He recognizes souls in human bodies are given the same guidance and protection he now sees clearly in the spiritual realm.

Can you paint?

"Yes, I can choose to do this and I will when I'm given the opportunity to rest. Guides work hard and there will be rest periods when I'm allowed to pursue my own interests."

Edmund has been put to work learning to be a guide. Saint Germain says guides devote themselves lovingly to the soul they watch and protect.

Describe painting there as it compares to here on earth. For instance, can you smell the paint?

"Yes, I feel the support (canvas) and smell the paint. The senses we had in a physical body are enhanced here. It is not a smell coming from the nose or olfactory tissues, but much deeper. For instance, a rose, is smelled as if one is united or merged with the flower."

Have you traveled to the land of Ireland which you love dearly?

"Yes, I live there – in the spiritual essence of the place. It was explained to me how all dense physical worlds are overlapped by a spiritual body. This is the same with us. I am seeing the lighter essence of all the places I love."

We also have spiritual bodies that overlap our dense physical form. Edmund is saying and comparing that with the fact that all places or countries have a spiritual body is well.

I want to clarify this spiritual body you speak of. Does it feel real?

"Yes, real and tangible but in a higher vibration."

Have you seen your Akashic Record?

This is the record of all our life-times stored in the spiritual world.

"Yes, it was at the first meeting with my elders. I was introduced to my higher selves in other past experiences prior to this one as Edmund. I will work in the higher levels as a teacher; to be a guide first, later to follow the ascension path."

Do you have a place to live?
"I have a small cottage; a place to call my own and contemplate my lessons."

Where in Ireland have you chosen to locate your cottage?

He laughed and said, "North of Dublin; close to St. Malachy and the life I had and loved in this part of the country."

Do you eat or drink anything?

"I have no need for bodily functions. There are too many other exciting experiences here."

When he answered no to my question about eating and drinking it's a good example of an older soul who has no interest in replicating the prior physical experience.

He continued to say, "This personal experience of transition tells us to never be afraid. Try to see the transition as a positive cycle in your life. We are all at different places or levels in this unfolding drama of life and death. Enjoy your physical experience; make the most of it in respect to your spiritual understanding of the whole. Do not focus all of your energy on the unimportant things. Be in union with God and Creator. Love yourself and give unconditional love to others."

6 THE JOURNEY

"If you would indeed behold the spirit of death, open your heart wide into the body of life. For life and death are one, even as the river and the sea are one." Kahlil Gibran

The extended journey refers to all possibilities awaiting our souls over the long-term stay on the other side. I asked Saint Germain if the mind travels with us when we die. Saint Germain answered as mentioned earlier in the book, "The mind is part of your overall consciousness. All your experiences are stored in the part of the mind you call the sub-conscious. When the mind travels with you to the higher energies here, it is an expanded mind. You are able to understand all aspects of your experience both in and out of the body. This is unveiled for those who can handle the information."

I wondered if the mind and consciousness were the same. He answered, "Yes, indeed. The brain is the physical container of all events, memories, and activities of the human experience. Your consciousness is outside of the brain within the medulla oblongata. This is the temple of the soul."

Is it true our memories of the last life fade? Are they like a dream?

Saint Germain said, "Yes, All your memories are gathered together and placed within the record of all your physical experiences. Then you become an expanded self; more than one body and one mind, but the collection of the whole as you have experienced physical life through the ages."

Are we taught how to retrieve information in our subconscious or does this information come up spontaneously?

Saint Germain said, "For most souls the information becomes available when it can be useful. There are younger souls who require guidance in seeking and using the memories."

Do we experience a period of amnesia after transitioning from body to spirit?

Saint Germain said, "This is based upon your soul's personal needs. Some souls must be given time of quiet and rest without the memories. When one has suffered a terrible death, and this event has harmed the soul, we give this soul a period of amnesia."

Are souls who are considered average placed together in war-torn lands or poverty-stricken countries? This seems harsh to me?

Saint Germain said, "No, this is not the way souls are distributed. It is much more complicated than this. Souls are combined in various parts of the world so each will fill the others up with whatever they lack. It is loosely designed to create balance, Souls who have lived numerous lives in the East, are encouraged to live in the West, and vice versa. It is arranged to provide the soul with the maximum amount of learning. The same is true for the outer planets. It is an attempt to achieve balance."

"When we leave the physical body what kind of body are we given in exchange?" Saint Germain said, "It is a light body. It is able to move by thought. It does not need food. The internal organs are absent." I asked him if I could open and close my hands using this light body." He laughed at me and said, "The hands work." He felt a need to show me and I could see him energetically on the other side moving his hands. He went on to say we will have a brain and a consciousness but an expanded consciousness.

Are we allowed to see everything existing within our total consciousness?

He said, "It is a selective process based on what each person can handle."

Do we wear clothing?

"Yes, it is created by you. There are cloaks on the teaching levels. These designate a soul's progress. On the physical levels one chooses attire that is familiar." He went on to tell me that I would wear a robe which would designate my soul group and my role as an instructor. The cloaks are different colors based upon a soul's level of spiritual advancement. I asked him if he planned to put me to work as a teacher and he said, "Yes indeed, you are a talented teacher and will work hard to assist souls."

I asked if telepathic communication exists on the other side. If so, what if everybody's talking at the same time?

Saint Germain was amused. He said, "I understand you are asking about mind to mind communication. This is the type of communication used on the other side." What was surprising to me is to learn what he said next and I quote,

"It is possible to communicate this way in our current life's journey." Of course I responded with a question. "How do we do this?" He answered me by saying, "Simply think the thoughts you would speak and watch the results." He went on to say some individuals would not pick up the thought but there are some who would hear it. He encouraged me to experiment with this and when I was successful in transmitting a thought to someone who responded, I would know I was dealing with one of the old souls. I thought this was fascinating.

I wondered if Disembodied Souls had the ability to make their family and friends feel them on their physical bodies- Like a feather that rubs against one's face.

Saint Germain said that this ability to reach into matter from the higher vibrations is given to some souls. They are older souls who are moving into the light. I told Saint Germain I had read about a soul who had left his physical body through suicide. "Could someone who had left his life through suicide be able to manipulate matter?" His answer was surprising to me and he said, "Yes, it is possible as some souls who commit suicide do so in an attempt to simply return home." I asked, "Won't this adversely affect the soul? He said, "Not always." Each soul is a unique combination of experience both good and bad. It is not common for someone who is an evolved soul to commit suicide but not impossible."

I asked, "Does the spiritual body resemble the physical body we had in the last life?" In the Tibetan book of the dead it says that we awaken to a new form which is not composed of matter.

Saint Germain said, "It looks like a body you have loved. You will choose a body from the many bodies which have carried you through your physical lives. Your favorite becomes your vehicle here. Most souls choose the last body, but you will have many options and will think carefully about the choice. This body moves by thought."

Does the light body need care?

"Yes, one's light is energy. It is through the soul and mind one cares for this energy. Do you not do this now?" I answered, "Yes, or else I would be tired." He responded, "It is the same. One does not have unlimited energy. One's light body does not require food; however, it does require rest." He went on to say, "Some souls have heavy dense energy, and others have lighter energy." Saint Germain said "We feel the difference in others energy when we are in a physical form. I agreed with him. He said the same is true here. He said, "When an Ascended Master, for instance, meets a soul on the first platform following death; there is a step downward into heavier energy. In other words, even in heaven there are gradations of energy from the first platform to the higher levels of vibration."

Do we eat food?

"Yes, food is available and one's memories provide the flavor. He went on to say we must be familiar with the taste because it is the memory of the taste that we experience." I was told the memory is very powerful and we carry all our memories of both our conscious and subconscious minds. I wondered if the taste was satisfactory and I was told yes and to remember the mind is powerful.

I asked Saint Germain, How much of earth's experience do we see after we leave. For instance, do we see social change, political change and all the new things happening on earth? For example, it will probably be unnecessary for people to drive their own cars in 25 years because cars will drive themselves. Will we be aware of new technology?" He said, "In the moment of crossing over a younger soul's desire to understand what is going on back on earth is still strong. The same souls ask, how do I communicate with loved ones? They wish to know the outcome of unfinished business. This is handled by those who guide the soul through the initial transition from body to soul. Later, this desire to know what has transpired on earth will diminish as the spiritual world is full of activities to enjoy.

He went on to say there is much to be accomplished in heaven and all earth activities fade until the moment of re-birth.

He said, "Souls preparing to return to a planet are informed of changes which have happened on the Particular planet since their last lifetime in that place."

How do we check on our loved ones on earth when we are in our spiritual bodies in heaven?

"It is done in the library where one's record of lives is stored. There is a small portal, similar to your computer.

One looks in and can see a summary of lives for the soul in question. You do not see the actual moment. It is a historical record. I asked Saint Germain, "Do many people look back? One of the stories in this book features a gentleman who said he doesn't want to know what is going on back on earth." Saint Germain said, "Very few souls want to look back. Many decline the opportunity. Life here is very full and one does not need to look backwards."

The Senses

I asked St. Germain if we hear, feel, taste and see. Do we use senses as we do in the physical world? Do these go with us when we die?

Saint Germain said it was a complex question but replied, "There are some senses attached to the body, and others to the soul." I love what he said next and I quote,

"In spirit you will see, but no earthly eyes are needed. In spirit you will hear but no words will be spoken. In spirit you will taste, but it is generated from memories. These memories exist in your mind."

"One experiences what is required. Some need the senses, particularly young souls. Most souls rapidly assimilate upwards from sight, touch, hearing, and smell to a more refined version of this. One must be present here to understand. For now this information is buried in your subconscious."

I asked him, "Are you saying we have no eyes to see? He answered me by saying, "yes, one perceives the energy. Energy is vital here. It is tangible. You will always recognize a soul's energetic imprint because each is unique. The eyes are connected to the soul; not to the form.

94

I commented, this is great for seeing people, but how do you "see" the ocean, birds, roses, that you have never seen before? Memory doesn't help here?

You will remember how to see spiritually instantly upon your arrival here. One sees it all as there is spiritual vision. You will understand when you arrive and see the clarity of the images. The soul is remarkable. It does not need a dense body here in the higher vibrations."

I asked about feelings; "Do we have physical feelings?" He said, "You will not feel as you experience it in a human body. Here there is a current; a strong energetic form which has substance but not in the way you sense the human body." Saint Germain said, "Everybody appears to be 25 years old and this is particularly true on the lower levels."

In heaven, there are different levels, or what Saint Germain refers to as the layers of the cake. Souls who live on the lower levels are still interested in the human experience and so have created younger bodies. Souls who reside at the higher levels are less interested in human bodies and instead, focus on their souls. That being said, the real way of recognizing another loved one is by recognizing their soul. In a human body we don't relate on a soul level however, when we die we do connect with the human soul.

I asked him to explain the sensation of touch and he said, "You will feel and this feeling transcends the physical experience as the vibration of all energies are higher here." I complained by saying, "I wish I could remember my previous memories of life on the other side while living now in this physical body." He understood my frustration and said, "The sum of all past memories would slow down your experience in the physical life." He went on to say, "In the more mature years, when we get older, some memories of the afterlife are shown to us because the lessons have already been mastered."

Do we have the use of our senses when we are on the other side?

"Yes, in fact, senses are enhanced on this level of vibration, to the extent, many are overwhelmed by the sounds and smells and music which permeates all levels of what you might call heaven." I asked, "If souls on the lower levels, those who have committed crimes in the body, would also have access to these senses?" Saint Germain said, "Yes, these souls have a deep need of the sounds and the scents. Many sleep and are soothed through the senses. It brings comfort in an experience of hard work involving revisiting past lives and actions; and I should say lack of actions as well."

Is there thought transference on the other side?

"This is a very complicated question. The ability to communicate is faster and more efficient here. Most use thought transference here but only if you choose to do so. One cannot hide thoughts as one can words. On the higher levels where higher learning takes place, choice is always to communicate internally. You will choose this when you come back—(he was referring to me). Most souls simply take comfort in using their senses."

Can we swim on the other side?

When I asked this question he laughed and said yes, "If you choose. You will re- visit places you have loved where bathing was done. You will feel the substance of water differently; more profoundly. It will be water magnified tenfold in its purity and softness. Bathing is a remedy for many souls who require its healing properties." I reminded him water was a physical substance. He said, "Yes, but water on this side has properties beyond the water you are familiar with on earth."

Are there seasons and can I see trees?

"Yes, more beautiful than you can imagine. The trees are alive here. This life is seen on the surface and one can bask in the energy of this tree. This form is created to comfort those who have loved nature. Remember, you create your reality, and what you create in the higher vibrations of heaven surpasses earth forms."

Rules in Heaven

I asked if there were rules in heaven and Saint Germain said, "There are unspoken rules at every level. There are guides who work with each soul to assist them in acclimating to the new environment. Just as I would adjust to a new place following a change of residence, the same is true in spirit. All is very carefully planned and those who need assistance are given personal attention and love."
I wondered if we would be able to look back and see what

was happening on earth. For instance, what progress had been made in medicine, or space exploration? Saint Germain said this, "there is a desire to know these things early in the experience here. It is logical to wonder and ask these questions. Eventually, any interest in the world of form is completely released. Life is full and exciting here. One would not waste time looking backwards."

Our Personal Interests on the Other Side

We do get to enjoy all the activities we loved on earth while we are in heaven. I asked Saint Germain if I would be able to create art in a place that is non-physical. I am an artist and I love to design and execute paintings in watercolor. It is something I am passionate about. I often think to myself, How will I die and leave my art behind? Saint Germain had a good laugh and he responded to me by saying, "I have heard your thoughts and you may relax. Should you choose to engage in the creation of art it will be available. All souls continue to enjoy their hobbies and interests." I responded, "what about supplies. You are talking about a nonphysical environment?"

Saint Germain responded, "Your joy is joy to me. Thoughts create the materials and you are encouraged to be in engagement with everything and everyone you love." I responded, "What about retaining my artwork. Can I keep it or does it disappear?" He responded, "This is a choice. You may create a gallery of your art for others to enjoy. If you decide to engage in other activities you may keep your art or delete the energy and later begin anew."

I asked him about music. Would people who love music and play instruments continue to play?

He said, "Of course. Just as you love art there are people who write and perform music."

Hearing this gives me great comfort. We are allowed to express every aspect of ourselves. All threads of past experience are offered to us so we will understand the entirety of our soul. He continued to say we choose the activities we want to experience and all the information is provided instantly by our thoughts. He took this opportunity to remind me how important our thoughts are. Here in the physical world we manifest our lives just as we do on the other side, but on the other side the thoughts manifest instantly. It may seem impossible to us now, but our ability to bring about instant manifestation will come back to us rapidly in heaven.

Churches

I wondered if people practice religious beliefs on the other side. Is there a church experience?

Saint Germain said there is every denomination represented here. We allow souls to worship as they wish, and yet we teach that all religions are one.

Visiting other Planets from the Other Side

We can visit other planets on the other side. Saint

Germain said it is often the first desire of the soul who is released to journey. What he means by journey is being allowed to move around in this new location and to have experiences in other places. He said, "The other worlds are like playgrounds of fun as compared to the earth. When we remember the places we visited on earth we are instantly there. I asked him if this would be unsettling and he said, "No, it is very comforting. All that is required is an effort to remember. You may remain as long as you like."

Handling all the Choices

I believe it will be difficult to handle the vast number of choices available to us on the other side. He told me this was very individual. He commented, "You might enjoy the experience but another could feel caught in a world of opportunity that shifts and changes through thought. Navigating through such an experience can be challenging. Younger souls want to feel the dense energy of the earth. Older souls are comfortable remaining in the higher and lighter realms for long periods of time." He went on to say the souls who love the higher vibrations desire to linger. In other words, they must be encouraged to reincarnate and continue on their soul's journey. This made complete sense to me. I have found this to be true in my own work. During my readings I see many souls who have lingered for well over 200 years on the other side. They are reluctant to jump back into a body. I asked Saint Germain how we manage time so we are able to meet all of our obligations. Saint Germain said, "It is a difficult question because there is a subtle way in which we are reminded of our responsibilities and obligations. He said "There is a subtle signal that is sent from our teachers telling us that it is time for us to gather."

I asked Saint Germain, "Can I eat chocolate on the other side. Tasting is a sense and wouldn't that be absent? He thought my question was very humorous and he laughed and said, "Yes, we see your love for chocolate. Your mind will instantly create this." I responded, "Is the chocolate very good?" He said, "Not the same, but very acceptable." I continued to question him about the use of the senses making the comment that we don't have the same human senses of smell and taste; is this not correct? He replied, "Yes, not in a human way. Your senses here are enhanced you see. A piece of chocolate is like the sum of five of your favorite chocolates all in one."

Planning steps to return to a human body

When it is time to start looking ahead to a return to the physical experience, the Elders will call a soul forward and request an audience (meeting) to discuss the next life. This is the first step. The soul is often surprised and not ready to discuss a return to a physical body. Saint Germain says very few want to have this discussion.

The Elders will explain the reasons for moving forward. Once the soul agrees, and this is necessary in respect to free will, the planning begins. First there is a decision made on gender. Many questions are asked such as what does the soul need, which souls from previous lives need to be encountered in the next life experience, what geographic location is preferred. It resembles a large jigsaw puzzle in which the pieces have to fit together. Our Elders are diligent in creating the blue-print of the next life. A list of tasks and a list of possible connections with other souls are created. There is a discussion about body characteristics and the soul is asked about their preferences. For instance, what has been missing in previous lives? What are your goals and ambitions? This information is combined with the Elders plan.

Then, there is a second stage where options are discussed. The elders project possibilities such as possible families, ethnic origin and places. Saint Germain says," "Think of your own experience when you search for a new home. You must consider the size, location, neighbors, climate, and if you have small children the type of schools available. The same level of thought is required to look towards a future life. These are the possibilities and it is like previewing a movie in which you say, "Yes, this looks good, or no, I do not desire this experience right now, or can I have it later please?"

I asked Saint Germain if we could choose an early death." He said "Only if this decision would contribute to our own growth, or if our soul needs to learn self-sufficiency, build character or benefit through loss."

Our Elders allow us to look at four or five life choices and the soul is given more time to consider the possibilities before the last meeting with them. Saint Germain said, "We make the choice and narrow down the selections." He said, "The Elders show you the possibilities and it is like designing a roadmap. Detours and roadblocks are shown to you. The choices are narrowed to two after all the probabilities; both good and bad are shown to us. Once a soul decides on a plan there is a final gathering to discuss the birth. One must wait until there is a body available and then the departure is discussed."

I asked, "What is it like to enter the body of the fetus or baby?" Saint Germain said, "It is the same as dying. There is a tunnel which is the reverse of death but the soul simply enters through the umbilical cord. Whether the soul enters at the solar plexus or brain depends upon the timing. Souls who enter the body early go through the umbilical cord. Those souls that enter late enter through the brain."

I asked a personal question. "There was a point in my life when I was recovering from a divorce and at the same time becoming involved in an abusive relationship. One day I was caught between the old relationship which was ending and the new one which was just beginning but showing signs of problems. I was in a shopping mall and for two hours I walked in circles trying to decide what to do. I decided to continue with the new relationship." I asked Saint Germain "Was I at a cross road?"

(Crossroad means we are being directed by the other side).

His response to me was "Yes, indeed all souls have moments in their earthly experience where deep decisions must be made. It is what we would call a little prompt or life's crossroad. At these critical moments, memories of seeing this moment from the spiritual platform prior to birth are felt in the emotional centers. In this moment you are reminded to make the correct decision based upon your prior educational decisions and plans for the life."

He went on to say they did not want me to return to my first husband and I was kept in the dysfunctional relationship in order to learn powerful lessons. He asked, "Do you agree?" I answered "yes."

This relationship which only lasted five years taught me some of the most powerful lessons in my life, and prepared me for the work I do today.

Organized Religion

I asked Saint Germain to explain the damage caused by organized religion in respect to the teachings about death and in particular the traditional heaven and hell teachings?

He responded saying, "Religion has engendered fear in some, and comfort for others. Much depends on the deeper understanding of the soul. Those who are young souls accept the teachings of the church and expect death to lead to either heaven or hell. They will create what they expect. However, they quickly wake up to the truth. There is relief when one realizes life continues here and later to be followed by incarnation into new bodies."

A Personal Story
David

Death is our sister, we praise Thee for Death
Who releases the soul to the light of Thy Gaze?
And dying we cried with the last of our breath
Our thanks and our praise. St. Francis of Assisi

This is a story about a man named David. He was very
successful and had a thriving business. He had everything
life could offer including a wife and two children. He was
very well-liked. He became involved with drugs and
alcohol. He overdosed and died at the age 62 losing
everything. He was a good man and did lots of great things
in the community to help people. Five days before he died
he saw his parents who had been dead for 30 years. He
freaked out.   The final blow was that his electricity was
shut off in the middle of winter. He was found in his bed
dead and holding a bottle of rum.

Saint Germain said, "It wasn't his social status and wealth
that led to his death." He said, He was a young soul and
even though at one time in his life he had everything
money could buy, he still felt empty. This is the case with
this individual." He went on to say, "He tried to use social
status to fill himself up but nothing would suffice."

.

What could the people around have done to help?

"The family chosen for this soul was carefully selected. The children were old souls."

Did loss of his earthly possessions cause his death?

"No, it was the loss of his soul."

Did he feel helpless?

"Yes, one feels helpless when he or she does not remember the lessons. Many angels assisted, and yet the soul was consumed by his need for love. He is now being assisted by many teachers here."

Did he choose to die?

"Yes, he was fighting his conscience to stay as he was afraid his family, particularly the children, would not be able to cope. When he arrived here he was greeted by the Elders and then sent to a very special place for rehabilitation for souls like him."

7 SOUL GROUPS

The mind is no more in the body than music is in the instrument.
Robert Alton Wilson

How many spiritual classrooms are on the other side?

Saint Germain said, "There is a vast hierarchy here. It is so intricate I cannot fully share the details with you." The soul group is the essence of where most hard work takes place between lives. It is also a place for personal encounter and relationships with other souls like you. The leader of each group is an evolved soul chosen for the group. There is much discussion and activities along the lines of resolving past difficulties and challenges. It is an opportunity to clear up the past and prepare for the next experience."

"Every soul who transitions is assigned to a soul group overseen by the elders. The number of levels is vast. Some souls are preparing to stay and work here. Others must work on issues which held them back while on earth. All souls sharing a similar challenge will be placed together. It is through resolving these issues the soul grows and is allowed to ascend."

Ascension happens when the soul no longer has to reincarnate into a physical body. Their physical world lessons are over and they begin their spiritual journey upwards through a process called ascension.

I asked Saint Germain, "Do we receive help from our soul group while in a physical body? He told me "No. There is no active participation with a soul group while

107

Inhabiting a physical body." The soul group is constantly being designed and, as he puts it, re-energized on a continual basis to serve individuals who will be participants. In other words, a soul group is not static. It is constantly changing to accommodate our needs based upon our earthly experience. When we arrive on the other side we will form relationships with souls like ourselves who have the same spiritual interests. He said, "You will be part of a group of old souls who possess spiritual gifts including seeing and working with spiritual masters."

I wondered how many levels or classrooms are on the other side. He said, "Too many for me to say as the quantities are always changing. The higher worlds are composed of many souls. There is a constant coming and going. All runs smoothly just as water flows down a river. There is an ebb and flow to the formation and dissolution of the teaching arenas. Soul groups form and then dissolve gently and naturally like water flows."

He said "The soul groups have many names and the group itself chooses the name." I asked him "What was the name of my last group. He said, "I knew you were going to ask that question." The name of the group was, "The Chargers." He continued to say "It was a group very anxious to grow and enhance their spiritual gifts." I had a good laugh when he said that!

There are many layers in the spiritual world. Saint Germain has often compared them to the layers of a cake. I asked him, "How many layers there were? He said, "We do not count. There is a beautiful harmony in comparison to the harsher experience of physicality. All is organized at the highest level of truth and beauty."

I wondered what the topics of discussion would be in a soul group. He responded by saying, "The topics are far-reaching; from personal experience to the eternal one. There is a leader, or in the case of older souls, many masters coming into the group to establish a topic and lead the discussion." I asked, "Is there someone actually speaking? Do we hear their voice, or is it mind to mind communication?" He said, "It is through the mind. In the beginning, in the less advanced groups, the leaders will speak so words can be heard, but this is not efficient."

I asked about souls who had lived difficult lives and done terrible things to other people. "What would the soul group experience be like for them?" He said, "These souls are not ready to maintain a group association. They are in a one to one arrangement with those trained to re-educate them towards the path of love. Once ready, they enter a level of what you might call kindergarten."

Explain what heaven looks like?

"It looks like any other place in the universe however the difference is your ability to create the environment you choose. There is a lack of solidity to this place. One's thoughts create heaven instantly. On earth or other dense planets the thought creates the design however one has a sense of delay in the arrival of the desire. "

The Akashic Record Library

"The Akashic Record Library is a huge area here in heaven. All lives are recorded. Many souls manage the library. Very few souls are allowed to see the complete history of their physical experiences with the exception of those who are ready for Ascension. The memories are returned based upon the soul's ability to comprehend them and learn from the experience. One is allowed a key to certain lives and not to others. There are those who manage the data. It looks like a library. Some souls use it as a library with real books and others prefer the tablets. There are small areas with chairs and desks so you might review a past life. This is similar to watching television. It can be seen thousands of times. Then, you are asked to describe the lesson to your teachers."

Why is there a need for chairs or desks?

Saint Germain said, "There is no need except for your comfort in having these objects. They are familiar and you will create what is comfortable for you instantly. All souls create an environment from their enormous memories."

I asked about myself and he said, "You will see your records upon your return to spirit." He said, "A teacher will sit with you as you look at the most difficult moments of your physical lives." He went on to say, "It is all handled with love and care for the soul is precious to us here. We wish to preserve and protect the soul. This is who you truly are."

A Personal Story

"The reality of my life cannot die, for I am indestructible consciousness," Paramahansa Yogananda

Michael S.

This gentleman lived alone in his own apartment. He died in his late 50s. He was found two days after his death in his apartment having died from a heart attack over the weekend. He had visited the hospital on a Friday evening. The doctors wanted to admit him because he had severe heart problems. Instead of being admitted to the hospital he went home to his apartment. There was some thought by the family that he was concerned about the expense and decided not to let them admit him. He died over the weekend and was found in his apartment by a man who worked with. Saint Germain assisted me in having this conversation. He was my x-husband.

Your voice sounds exactly like it did when you were living. Did you try to contact me after you died?

(The weekend he died I was having all kinds of strange experiences. At this time nobody knew that he had died. I felt very out of sorts and unable to get anything done. I was finding myself surrounded by monarch butterflies everywhere – even in heavy traffic where I lived in the state of Maryland. I had to spend the night with my mother in another town and in the middle of the night I was woken up by the chiming of an old clock that has been in our family for over 100 years. It doesn't work, but it did that night! It woke me up at 1 o'clock

111

AM and 3 o'clock AM. My mother didn't hear it because she's deaf. In the morning I asked her if she had the clock fixed and she said," Oh no, the clock hasn't worked for at least 50 years! "At the time I didn't know that Mike was trying to get my attention. Two days later I heard that he had died.

Here is Michael's response;

"Yes, I did try to get somebody's attention. I was in difficulty – not understanding my situation just after my death. I stayed with my body but I didn't know I was dead. I saw the body on the floor but I was still okay. It was so confusing. Finally, a gentleman came into my apartment. I asked him how he got in. I didn't feel threatened by his presence, just confused. He told me I had died and that he was here to bring me home. I was still confused, but he was so warm and loving."

What did he look like?

"He was very tall and had a long robe – it was cream-colored; simple, and he had a belt around his waist."

What happened next?

"In a flash; we were standing in a circle – like a city plaza with marble everywhere. My grandfather and grandmother were there. I remember them from my childhood. I was relieved to be here. I worried about my children and family. Also – who would take care of my body-- I died so fast."

You realized you were dead?

"Yes."

Why didn't you admit yourself to the hospital when you are encouraged to do so by the doctors?

"I didn't have the money and I really wasn't concerned about myself. Maybe I did want to die?"

Saint Germain has told me many times that we choose the moment of our death. I believe he did choose his moment.

Have you worked with your elders to look at your life?

"Yes, I reviewed every detail of my life from age 1 to my death at age 59. I was shown the good and the bad – the feelings and emotions of myself plus the emotions of others who I affected by my actions."

Were you able to bring any closure to that life?

"Yes, it was very difficult to see. I made many mistakes. I never felt worthy of my family, friends, and children. I felt disappointed in the choices I made. Now, I am thinking about a new life and reversing all the mistakes."

Do you look in on our children?

"If I want to see them it is possible, but I have no desire to look back. This life has faded. I am keeping busy with classes and meetings with the elders and friends. There is a full schedule here."

Jane's note-- I have heard this before – that someone who has crossed over is not interested in looking back to earth. It seems to be a common sentiment.

Do you think you were an alcoholic?

"Yes, I was. It was a way of blotting out the world and not facing myself. I was weak. Please forgive me. I realized how right you were about the expanded life that is unseen. Now I have been able to confirm this."

I thanked him for speaking to me. He commented he loved me and the children and we would see each other again.

8 THE LESSONS

Just as thoughts create our reality here — so this is true with our death — decide now how to think of death. Saint Germain

Meeting our other personalities

This was always a big question for me. Consider all the hard work involved in acquiring many skills and talents during a lifetime. Then, we grow old and after years and years of struggle we become competent in a number of things and it's time for us to go. Saint Germain says we don't lose anything when we die and return home. In fact, we have an opportunity to meet our expanded self. He says this is the totality of who we are. He uses threads as a metaphor and says we are composed of many threads. They are a part of recent and past experiences. When we reside in a physical body we are continuously tapping into the knowledge. When we cross over into the spiritual world we are introduced to the threads of other lifetimes based upon what we can handle. He continued to say we would never be burdened with data from thousands of lifetimes, but we are taught to see our previous experiences either as a singularity or as a whole. In other words, we can look at all of the threads we are allowed to see, or we can look at the single thread of a particular life.

If we have made the transition from physical to spiritual lives many times we will understand the integration of other experiences or threads and it will feel very natural. He says younger souls are more challenged by this experience. Older souls have already assimilated aspects of their soul in previous trips in and out of the body. He says, "Some of your embodied experiences have already been dealt with and therefore there is no need to revisit these lessons. The focus remains on embodiments with remaining challenges."

I asked if we have an immediate down load of all of this data when we make our transition to the other side and he said, "No, not immediately. First there is a life review followed by a session with your elders. During this meeting, part of the experiences are opened up to your consciousness. Much discussion takes place. An expanded consciousness is given to you based upon your readiness. Some are anxious to have all the threads revealed, and others find the process difficult." He went on to say, "While we exist in our physical bodies we have a sense of these threads coming in and out of our consciousness. This is what we refer to as 'de ja vu'. We often receive a true sense of knowing about an event, place, or person. Memories associated with the threads of past lives often slip into our dreams."

It is not the *experience* of a lifetime which is important but instead it is the lesson gained during the experience. A short life can be as valuable as a long one depending upon the lessons learned.

Do we choose the life lessons before birth?

"Yes, there is discussion and not everything is revealed in the early conversations. Some souls need to know very little to be successful in achieving mastery throughout the life ahead. Others are given more details and these souls receive many prompts to remember the turns in the road."

If there is a mass exodus of people like the Holocaust, do they come back in the same area? Do they study together on the other side?

"This is a very good question. There is an agreement to enter a body during a challenging period of history. They are informed they may be called to make decisions of faith or love; or to do the opposite, choose darkness and power. Some souls choose not to participate, and instead ask for lives with fewer trials. Remember, these souls will be prepared for any event for which they volunteered. While in spirit, they often gather together with souls who were part of the group energy of that particular event. They may decide to reincarnate together but it is their individual choice with the guidance of the elders. No soul is forced to do anything against their will."

Traveling on the other side

I wondered if it was possible to travel on the other side. Saint Germain's answer was surprising to me and this is what he said, "Yes indeed, there is an opportunity to re-visit places and events one has enjoyed in past lives. You will enjoy this experience as there is no pressure to travel, and the journey is controlled by your thoughts." He went on to say, "you will be able to travel with those you have known from previous lives, particularly souls who have had experiences in the same physical place as yourself." Saint Germain continued, "There is a purpose to the travel as one must revisit past experience to re-learn the lesson. Re-working the lesson in trying it another way. It is an opportunity to change the energy of the past to affect the current moment and those future events awaiting you." He went on to say this is a difficult concept to explain as you are still in a human body. Basically, the present and past bump into each other." Saint Germain says, "You will see the past experience and current activities on the stage of life all happening together. You will feel both your past and present colliding."

I repeated this to make sure I understood it, "We learn from our past by revisiting it. Then we see and act differently to affect our larger soul? He confirmed by statement. "It's important to mention if we have not experienced a previous life in a particular place, a return journey back would be impossible. We have to visit or live in a place while in a physical body in order to go back to it when we are in spirit."

So I asked another question, "If I lived in Japan in 10 AD will I see that time as if it existed in my previous experience or life, and I would also see the modern time period as well? Is this correct?"

Saint Germain said, "You will see both – 10 AD and the current energy of the present. It is a merging of both and you will be satisfied with this energy. All time lines intersect; crossing over into the present. You cannot handle this experience while in a physical body; however, within your spiritual body all is possible. Just as all threads cross over and create a tapestry of your experience, the same is true in traveling here to places you desire to see again and experience. "

I continued, "So we also revisit events and situations from a past life needing to be changed in order that we can grow? I used as an example a difficult moment in a previous marriage." I was in the middle of moving my home from Virginia to Maine and my husband began screaming and yelling at me and the movers. It was something I will never forget and I wondered if that kind of a moment could be seen again and handled in a different way."

Saint Germain said, "In a personal situation such as this it would be carefully reviewed by the leaders of your soul group. The leader of your soul group would speak to the leader of the ex-husband's soul group. They would decide if a joint exercise would be useful." Saint Germain points out, "One soul might be ready to release and change the moment, but the other may not be ready." He continued to say, "We are encouraged to re-enter the spiritual classroom with souls who are at the same level of understanding as ourselves so we can better understand the events of a physical life." He mentioned, "There are instructors who monitor our progress. Some of the events we have left in physical time are deeply painful and it can take hundreds of attempts to release the energy." I commented, "This sounds like very hard work?" He responded, "In your physical lives you are in the classroom. Here, in spirit you are also in the classroom, but fully aware of it. <u>In the physical experience, very few souls understand they are engaged in lessons every moment.</u>"

Returning to a physical body

It is difficult for some souls to leave the spiritual world. The elders often push a soul back into the physical experience. I asked, "Could you explain the process by which souls are prepared to return to a physical life?"

Saint Germain said, "There is a discussion regarding soul's plan. What does the soul need? Which souls from previous lives must be encountered? It is a large jigsaw puzzle. The pieces must fit together. The elders are diligent in the design of the blueprint. The soul is then asked about their preferences. It is important to identify what may be missing from previous lives? What are the soul's goals and intentions? This information is combined with the elder's plan. Then there is a stage where options are discussed. Think of yourself when buying a new home. You must consider the size, location; neighbors, climate, and the schools, do you not?

I answered, "Yes of course."

He continued, "So you see it is the same, however, the elders are able to project scenes outward to you. These are possibilities and outcomes similar to previewing a movie. You have the opportunity to say "Yes, this looks good," or "No. I do not desire this experience now; but perhaps later please."

I asked, during the planning, is the possibility of an early death considered?

He responded, "Yes, one might choose early death for their own growth or for another soul who needs to learn self – sufficiency, or build character through loss."

I asked, "How many lives are considered?"

Saint Germain said, "The choices are narrowed down to two and then the probabilities are shown to you – both good and bad."

I mentioned a very difficult marriage which lasted only five years. He replied, "All souls have moments during their earthly experience where an important decision must be made. This is a life's crossroad. At these critical points, memories of seeing this moment in time from the spiritual platform before birth are felt in the emotional centers. You are encouraged to remember and to make the correct decision based upon your educational plans here. We did not want you to return to your first husband. You were kept in this marriage to learn powerful lessons. Do you agree?

I asked St. Germain, "Are we given a little prompt about upcoming events in our life through our dreams?" He said, "Yes, of course. You are out of your body when dreaming. Do you understand? Your deeper consciousness provides you with lessons and symbols of what lies ahead."

I replied, "I thought we slept when we arrived in heaven?" Saint Germain replied, "Yes. Immediately upon arrival, but also in intervals of your own choosing. Even non-embodied spirits enjoy rest, quiet, and contemplation. "

"Do all souls, regardless of the planet they have lived on, arrive at the same place?" He said, "All souls return to the spiritual world with consciousness and their astral bodies. You will shed the memory of the unique body very quickly and all souls relate to each other as non-physical beings. The old ones like yourself have had outer planet experiences and can quickly adjust. Physical bodies are unique but the soul is the same."

Saint Germain says, "We end up at the level that matches our vibration." I asked, "Are there seven astral planes?" Saint Germain said, "It is a difficult concept to convey; much easier to experience. Simply imagine a winding staircase and on each level one is encouraged to stay for a while and take the classes offered. There are many levels. Seven is simplifying a very complicated system. We might say this; the halls (meaning the areas containing rooms at the various levels) can be unlimited as a soul climbs the staircase. At the top one sees a panorama. At the bottom one's sight is limited. He went on to say some souls move rapidly upwards and others linger on a level equivalent to a lifetime on earth."

I asked, "Can an experience in the body be erased?" He said this was a complicated question and one you would understand more fully from the perspective of being in your light body. He said, "There is always a decision made by the Council of Elders regarding the process of returning a soul to the universal pool of substance. It is a serious matter. We attempt to save all souls."

The universal pool of substance contains the energy from which all souls are born.

I stated, "I have read about the chamber of colors and light healing? Is there such a place?" Saint Germain said, "It is a playground of sorts with light and color. One has the opportunity to play with the moving spectrum of colors and the light has the ability to heal wounds from the past. Most souls are encouraged to partake of this place and some are never tired of visiting the hall. There is a joyful quality to the non-physical realm."

I continued to ask for more information about this interesting place and Saint Germain said this, "It is a place of great comfort and recreation for many souls. It is immense as one cannot see the boundaries while being present within the energy. It is a healing arena and this is its main purpose. The light is warm and its essence is cleansing for the soul's light body. All emotions and fear are eliminated. One releases pent-up energies by engaging in sport with others."

A Personal Story

John H.
Born: October 5, 1959
Died: March 26, 2016

After Glow
*I would like the memory of me to be a happy one; I would like to
leave an afterglow of smiles when life is done.*

*I would like to leave an echo whispering softly down the ways, of
happy times and laughing times and bright and sunny days.*

*I would like the tears of those who grieve to dry before the sun, of
happy memories that I leave when life is done.*

Saint Germain introduced me to a man named John. He
died at the age of 55 after falling headfirst into a culvert on
the side of his apartment building. He had suffered his
entire life with substance abuse. He had struggled to stay
sober during the years prior to his death. His family was
unclear as to how he actually died. The body was found by
the police and there was a question about whether it was an
accident or someone had pushed him into the culvert.

**Thank you for allowing me to speak with you. How
did you die?**

John replied, "It was an accident. I was looking forward to
my new apartment and getting a job. I was feeling good the
afternoon of the accident. I put on my stereo headphones

to listen to some music. I was inside my apartment. I had just had surgery on my bad knee. I had pain medication for my knee and I took one pill. The knee became swollen and I took one more pill. I stepped out in the alley and someone called me. I looked up and didn't see anyone. I must have stepped towards the side of the house and lost my balance. All I remember is lying on a bed surrounded by people dressed in white. I thought this was the emergency room. I was so relieved but I couldn't remember how I got there. Someone came in and took my hands and said to me, "you are out of your body."

John continued to say, "I looked at my feet and arms and they looked the same to me. I was laughing and everyone else was also. They brought me a mirror and as I looked into the mirror I saw only light."

Were you scared?

"No, I was laughing. I couldn't stop laughing. The light became soft and I saw my father. He hugged me and told me I was okay. He said this was my new home now. I asked him, how did this happen? I don't remember how I got here."

Are you still breathing?

"Hell yes, It feels like nothing different."

He continued to share his story, and said he went to sleep soon after his arrival. He slept for about three months of our time here on earth.

I asked Saint Germain, "Was anything done for him during this period of sleep?"   He said, "No, it is time for a complete re-set of the soul. All fear and self-inflicted pain is swept away. Souls must be ready to participate in the De-briefing here without the shock of the death and transition."

I continued my conversation with John.

What did you do after you slept?

"I am spending most of my time with my group."

Can you describe this group and who is in it?

"I am with those who have had a similar death experience.--a sudden death without memory of what happened."

I asked, "Are they also people who have had previous problems with substance abuse or drug addiction?"

He replied, "No, that will come later."

Why did you choose this life in the first place?

"It was a last-minute decision. My father was my best friend from a previous life. I knew he would make this life experience safe for me. I have struggled through-out all my lives on earth. This is a better place. He laughed loudly."

What will you do now?

"I am going to talk, listen, rest and fish."

I asked, "Have you met your guides"

John – (Laughing) "There are many. I am never alone."

That's good right?

"It's okay but I want to think back."

I don't understand what you mean?

"To go over all the events of my life with my wife and kids."

Why can't you do that?

"It's not time and I'm not ready."

Has your guide said that?

"Yes. He said to wait and the right time will come. There is no hurry."

Do you eat?

"Yes, we have a large building with food and drinks. There is a lot of time to talk here."

What do you talk about?

"Our experiences before death."

He went on to tell me he had seen his mother; she died a few months following his death. He indicated she was in a different location in heaven. He said, "I am relieved she is here. I know I am not alone." I asked him if he was feeling a lack of love and he answered, "No, I feel love here but my mother is familiar."

A Personal Story

A Killer Dies

As I pass from this world to the next, I know that heaven or hell is determined by the way people live their lives in the present. The sole purpose of life is to grow. The ultimate lesson is learning how to love and be loved unconditionally." Elizabeth Kubler – Ross

I won't mention the shooter's name, but some of you may recognize the event I am referring to. In this event a single shooter seriously injured over 50 individuals who were attending a concert. He used automatic weapons and shot into the crowd from his hotel room from an upper floor close by. There were many deaths.

I asked Saint Germain, "Can you explain why someone would take the lives of so many? Was it because the person was mentally ill, or possibly possessed by an evil spirit? Saint Germain said, "I recognize how deeply disturbing this event was for many living in the United States who heard and watched the news on television." He said, "When something like this happens there is a reason unique to the soul. In other words, we can't make generalizations that somebody who does this is simply possessed, or mentally ill."

Saint Germain continued to say, "This soul was sick in mind and overcome by past karmic debts. You see, he was rehabilitated in spirit during many earth years of your time for having killed many in previous lives."

I believe St. Germain meant this man would have spent many years on the other side compared to the average soul. It was my impression the shooter had been a very bad person and had done something horrible in a previous life.

Saint Germain said, "He was not free to give me this particular information; however this event was deeply distressing to those who had released the soul to return to a physical life believing his past debts had been paid." He continued to say, the soul may never return to a body and is likely to be sent back to the the universal pool of substance. He said this is the energy of God and there are some souls who simply fall back into the "vibration of the whole." He continued to say, "One must release all past trauma before being allowed to return to a physical body. Success in releasing past actions makes it possible for some souls to return to the body quicker than others. Those who have suffered bodily and mental strife take longer to prepare for another life experience. Small aspects of trauma can be carried into a physical life if they serve the soul. Each situation is unique and is treated as such.

I asked, "Can a demonic entity take over a soul?" St. Padre Pio stepped forward to speak. He said, "Dear one and God bless you. Yes, but demonic entities are attracted to those of great purity – like me – as it is their desire to win over the souls of those who ascended into a deep union with Christ and the universal energy of love. This soul, and God bless him, has failed in his return to the experience of the physical life."

St. Padre Pio was a Catholic priest and a mystical Saint. He suffered through-out his life with the stigmata (wounds of Christ). Many healings are attributed to his intervention.

I wanted to know if this event had been anticipated by souls on the other side. Saint Germain said, "Yes it was anticipated. There had been attempts to stop the event by those who knew the intention of the shooter." He went on to say, "There were many angels and spiritual guides who were available in the crowd during the event to help the injured and dying souls."

10 YOUR QUESTIONS

"Death is nothing more than rearranging molecules on a physical level, and displacing consciousness from a vehicle in the enclosure to one of the free nature. Life has always been; life always is. There is no such thing as taking life, for life simply changes to another form." A disembodied spirit

How can everyday people communicate with their loved ones?

Saint Germain – "One must first believe the loved ones are receptive to your thoughts and love. Know as you think of your mother and father here, they feel the energy and love of your thoughts. Sending and receiving thoughts is not simply relegated to the physical earth. All your thoughts and feelings are felt by those in spiritual bodies. They know and are blessed each time you send them love and your memories of your time together. Take a moment in the morning and evening to speak to them. Know that they always receive your messages."

He continued, "You must understand you have a busy life on earth and your loved ones have the same here. When you connect with them, choose a time to make the connection. Perhaps, before you prepare to go to sleep. Send them love and do this at the same time each day. They will wait for you."

What damage has organized religion caused in our

understanding of life after death?

"Creation of fear in withholding the truth of everlasting life."

If I become enlightened in this lifetime and, upon being received in the spiritual world, do not reincarnate but decide to stay with God …. AND, if time does not exist in any but the earthly realm (thus, all time happens at once), what happens to the me that existed (exists) in all my life times?

Saint Germain said, "Your elders will decide if you are an Ascension candidate and on a path to enlightenment. The "you" always exists; however, it is an expanded self, containing the memories of all lives."

Do animals have souls?
"Yes"

Do we see our animals the minute we cross over?

Saint Germain laughed when I asked him this question. He said, "No, there is a process you see. You will be greeted by your guides and if necessary brought to one of the healing centers. Arriving here is like your hospital triage system and there are steps. We do not rush. All activity is driven by the needs of the soul and the circumstances of the death. There will come a time after one has rested and seen the elders in which animal and human connections are addressed. All past connections are active in the souls plan going forward into a new life."

Are there soldiers from wars still caught in the astral

realm?

"Yes, however all souls caught in this place are rescued. There are teams here trained for this duty."

Why is there such a thing as death?

"It is an opportunity to rest and to revisit one's lessons, goals, and to review achievements. If each soul would see life as a school it is very simple. After your studies there is a summer vacation before returning to the classroom."

How does free will affect the time and means of death? In particular, it is written, our days are numbered. Are they?

"You choose the time and the means of your death."

When can this choice be made? Can it be changed mid-life?

"You choose when you are ready. Your spiritual team will hear your thoughts. We are very aware of the soul's needs and desires."

Can I ask that this lifetime be my last, and be given some kind of a sign that it will be so?

"No, one cannot ask for this. However, one can become a high achiever. Take on the lessons and the obstacles on the path by exercising love in all decisions; extending a helping hand to those in need, and establishing bonds of love with non-physical guides and angels who love you and guide you. The physical earth is a large classroom. You are never given more than you can handle. However, some souls fail to achieve even a small part of their original plan. If one works hard and allows their spiritual team to assist, the return to one's spiritual home can be rapid. As such, one will not have to return to a physical body."

What are ghosts?

Saint Germain liked this question. He said, "There are non-physical; non-human lifeforms. There are souls who are caught in the astral plane. They have left the physical body but remain connected to matter. There are strong emotional ties to matter for some. They refuse to be assisted by those who are trained to rescue them and return them home."

Is there transportation in heaven?

"Yes, by thought."

Where is heaven?

Saint Germain said "It is everywhere you see; superimposed over all physical worlds. Think of this place like an egg. The outer shell is heaven and you are the yoke. The vastness of heaven cannot be described. The vibrations are immense and surround the universe. The understanding of the connection between the two is shared with souls who ascend. This is all I will say." I responded, "Are you saying it is not a place it is an experience?" He answered me by saying, "It is both. It is an experience; however, do you not have an experience on earth in dense matter?" I responded, "You are implying that it is vast in its scope?" He answered "Yes, we understand. Be still and ponder this vastness."

Do souls always have the ability to cross over, or do they need help sometimes?

"There are souls who desire the physical experience and hold on. There are angels who assist them in moving forward."

Are there gardens and libraries and animals everywhere?

"Yes – unlimited access to many beautiful places."

Will we reunite with those loved ones even if we've been rejected by them here on earth?

"Yes – all past relationships are re-visited. All rejection has to be fully explored. All parties partake of the discussions. Only love is acceptable. Past debts are always balanced."

It's important to remember, forgiveness is a gift we give ourselves. This is one of my favorite quotes from "The Course in Miracles."

When a pregnancy is naturally terminated early, or a baby soul does not make it during birth and delivery--- I believe it is the mother soul that chooses this very painful experience for the lessons learned through the loss of a child. The question is, "What happens to the child's soul? Does the child also accept this painful

experience and return to another's womb for delivery, or has the baby soul not been created yet?

"It is often the case of the child's hesitation. More work is necessary in planning the next life."

Does the soul know when it is time to die? Is there any acknowledgment in the conscious self?

"Yes, the soul tells us when they are ready, however many are unaware that they themselves have sent the signal. The signal says I am ready to come home. Many bury this knowing. It is too difficult to face. Those who accept the upcoming death and welcome it, have the best experience of leaving physical form and seeing fully the beauty of this place called home. One is always aware however of a subtle desire to leave. This may be surprising to the soul who arrives here and did not realize it was their wish."

Can we merge with our source and lose our unique personality?

"This occurs in certain rare circumstances. When a soul has been evil it sometimes is returned to the universal pool of substance. It is very rare. Attempt to rehabilitate a soul is always tried first."

Can we change our past actions?

"Yes, you re-enact the scenes again here in heaven. Some souls do this many times to change the energy of a prior event."

Can a soul in the afterlife leave?

"Yes, very good question. The soul can change their mind or be resuscitated, but when one crosses the gate there is no turning back. There is a gate that marks the boundary between the lower vibrations and the upper energies."

How do you get souls to return to a body after this incredible spiritual life?

"It is the only way to grow; to enter a physical form and continue to be challenged by life lessons."

Why is communication cut off when someone dies?

"This expression *cut off* is in the mind. All souls can communicate with their loved ones. Think of them often and send messages telepathically through your mind. Your mind is powerful."

Why does it take a spiritual medium to make the connection? Why the wall between the spiritual and physical?

"Spiritual mediums are older souls and have learned to manage the energies in these higher vibrations. All souls have the ability to reach upward and make connections with those who have departed the physical world. There is no wall except what your mind believes."

Why do some people seem to connect with close loved ones as they are dying – for an example having dreams about how they will die?

"These are souls who are very close to the one who is anticipating the transformation from physical body to spiritual body. There is telepathic communication between the two."

What about signs from the other side – butterflies, smells, and things being moved?

"Souls who leave this earthly realm will quickly learn the power of manipulating the higher energies here. They are counseled not to disrupt the lives of souls still serving out their human lives. Souls who cross over and discover this ability are trying to get your attention."

Can we hide things from people when we are in spirit?

"Yes, one still retains their privacy. Many souls in the higher energies are processing deep information. There are quiet places here for contemplation, study, and prayer. There is an expansion of how you see yourself, and therefore, many thoughts to process and many situations to understand. There is work here."

Is it possible to spend so much time and energy looking for ways to grow spiritually that we miss the actual opportunity? Or looking for answers about life or the afterlife. In other words, we spend so much time looking for answers to mysteries that we miss living the life we are meant to live here and now?

"One must seek balance. It is better to ask questions rather than to simply accept one situation as all which exists. Continue to be inquisitive as this is the mark of an old soul."

How long does it take to reincarnate?

"For some souls it may be a hundred earth years and for others it may be centuries. Each soul is unique, and so is their soul's journey from spirit to matter."

When we die, are we protected in the new experience?

"All souls, regardless of the manner in which they have died are protected and guided diligently by guides and angels."

Do our loved ones who have crossed over know our thoughts?

"This is possible however, souls on the other side are very busy, and as they begin to see themselves as the sum of all their former lives and experiences they look ahead, not back."

I am speaking of somebody who wants to leave – how come a lot of requests are not answered or fulfilled?

"Each soul is unique and has their own unique journey towards enlightenment. The elders know the content of the soul's contracts and so you must except that it is not possible to know everything."

How long are you in stupor--- does everyone go into it?
"Every soul has a unique experience."

My mother-in-law at death had a beam of light come out of her eyes. Then, she blinked and the skin on her eyes looked like a snake. Then she blinked again and her eyes were normal. She wasn't a nice lady in life.

"It was the way she viewed her soul. This was her creation. She saw what she believed."

Is there a spiritual connection between sickness and death, or are they two different ideas?

"They are both opportunities to choose a path. Sickness can lead to death if the soul chooses to see it that way. Every event in one's life is considered spiritual, for that is who you are – a spiritual being."

Is there any benefit to the deceased to have repetitive contact with those left alive? Are there any detriments?

"There are benefits in so far as it does not disrupt their own journey."

Does this contact create an energetic cording to the deceased and keep them from moving forward with their life review and evolution?

"No."

Do requests by the living for communication with those who have crossed over keep the deceased

energetically tied to the 3-D plane?

"No, the soul's guides and elders would never allow that to happen."

Can a person who has died and is in heaven move physical matter?

"Yes, there is a higher level of energy remaining after death. This is emotional energy, and it can be directed to cause a movement on the physical plane."

What about suicide?

"Those who commit suicide give up the physical experience. As a result, they miss many of the important lessons. It will be necessary for them to revisit the lessons and repeat them once again."

Does part of our soul stay in the spirit world when we incarnate here on earth

"Yes, many times a portion of the soul is left behind. The amount is determined by your Elders. They ask the question; how much soul energy is required in this life? What challenges await this soul?"

If so, is there still work with our soul group to further our progress towards perfection and ability to ascend?

"Yes, there is always work to be done with the soul group until one has been given the blessing to follow an ascension path. Even past this milestone there still remains work to accomplish at the higher levels."

Question – Can we find out our soul's name and the members of our soul group through life regression or connection to an Ascended Master?

"Yes, it is possible to learn your soul's name and see your connection to those who guide and serve you while you're in a physical body. The soul group is always changing; therefore, you will not know this until you leave your physical body."

There have been so many shootings in the United States and around the world using dangerous weapons. What does the spiritual world think of our gun laws and the right to carry and bear arms?

"It is a difficult issue on planet earth. Many civilizations have renounced all weapons including those nuclear base missiles which are unknown except on earth. It is deeply troubling to us, however, it will be many centuries before the weapons, and I mean any type of weapon, are removed from earth. It is fear which binds the man to his weapons. He does not realize God does not kill the soul. However, it does mean the one who shoots another has lost his soul."

What about someone who is defending their country and as a soldier he kills another human being. Does this affect his soul adversely?

"Defending one's country and fellow man is the work of the soul – to place one's personal and physical self in jeopardy. This is a gift to those one protects."

Please explain the phrase, "matter is frozen light here in the physical world."

Saint Germain said, "It is energy. You see it as frozen, but the molecules which make up the matter are constantly active."

Death equals energy separating from matter--- I'm not sure I understand this?

"Yes, one's soul departs. The soul is the energy and the body is the matter."

CLOSING REMARKS

I said to Saint Germain, "Death is our birthright, correct?" He replied, "Yes indeed. Death is necessary in order to accumulate experience; the experience of a physical environment grows your knowledge of who you are as an unlimited being. To avoid death would be stagnation. Just as birth is an exciting adventure, so is death, and the cycle continues."

I watched a wonderful movie this year called, *Let There Be Light.* It was a story about a family who lost a child. The father could not understand how God could have taken this child away from him and so he became an atheist. He preached his views of atheism all over the world. His wife, on the other hand, still retained her faith in God. The marriage came apart.

One day, the father, was in a serious automobile accident after becoming drunk. In the unconscious state he saw the child he had lost. He experienced a place of love and safety. He had the opportunity to say goodbye to this child.

The father recovered from the accident and began to ask questions about his near-death experience and seeing his dead son. He spent a lot of time with his family's minister. Eventually he renewed his faith and he and his wife were remarried.

As they were planning to renew their vows, his wife came down with an inoperable brain tumor. Her time was limited. They had two other children besides the one they had lost. The children understood their mother was not well.

One day, the children were in the living room, and the mother walked out of the room into the bedroom. Her little boy said, "Mommy, are you coming back here?" The mother thought this was an opportunity for a teachable moment. She said, "I am not sitting in the living room with you, and you cannot see me. Do you understand?" The little boy said, "Yes." The mother finished by saying, "just because you can't see me doesn't mean that I am not here."

Isn't this also true for the rest of us? Just because we can't see our loved ones with our open eyes, does not mean they are not here. The veil between physical and spiritual life is very thin. Just imagine your loved ones very close---in the other room.

Thank you for reading our book. I know Saint Germain will be pleased if only one reader is helped to see life as an eternal journey back to our true home with God.

Blessings, Jane *Halliwell Green*

ABOUT THE AUTHOR

Jane Halliwell Green has been able to hear spirit voices since she was a little girl. Her deeply religious intuitive grandmother was her mentor and taught her how to read the cards. Jane did readings for many years using Tarot cards. One morning she was woken up out of a deep sleep by a loud voice that said," Arise, arise, and hear the Clarion call, for one and for all." Jane was startled, but went into a meditative state and asked which spirit was trying to get her attention? Clairvoyantly, she saw herself taken to a high cliff overlooking the ocean. She says, "I could see myself walking up the steep steps to a cathedral with no roof. Standing at the entrance was a gentleman dressed in beautiful robes. He greeted me, and told me he was the Ascended Master Saint Germain. Saint Germain has lived many lives, but the one that most people are familiar with is his life as Joseph, the father of Jesus. He said we would be working together, and this included writing a book to help others. This current book about death is my third channeled book working with this great spiritual teacher.

Jane is a trance medium able to speak Saint Germain's words directly. She works with people all over the world doing readings and teaching spiritual development classes from her home in Ohio.

One day while working on this book Jane asked Saint Germain, "what is the meaning of death?" He answered her by saying this, "there is no special meaning. It is simply part of the evolution of one as a non-physical being, and the necessity of moving higher on the scale of understanding your connection with God-- meaning, the path of full return to the light, and ultimately to the service of humankind. You have experienced physical death hundreds of times yet do not remember. There is no blackness here except what you create yourself. The experience is gentle and most souls have left their physical shells many times. Simply release the fear and this will make the impending death very easy."

Contact Jane

Web-site: http://www.janehalliwell.com

E-mail: jane@janehalliwell.com

Do not stand on my grave and cry.
I am not there
I did not die

Made in the USA
Coppell, TX
02 December 2021

66930633R00089